JUSTICE AND HISTORY
IN THE OLD TESTAMENT

The Evolution of Divine Retribution
in the Historiographies of the
Wilderness Generation

by

Richard Adamiak

with a Foreword by David Noel Freedman

John T. Zubal, Inc.
PUBLISHERS AND BOOKSELLERS
Cleveland

Published in the United States of America
John T. Zubal, Inc.
Publishers and Booksellers

ISBN 0-939738-08-2

Foreword

Richard Adamiak has written a provocative and stimulating monograph on an important theme: "Justice and History in the Old Testament." It is a model of constructive scholarship, combining historical-critical investigation with serious theological insights, indirectly but forcefully responding to the numerous critics of our time, who argue that the one is ineffective and the other unacceptable, thus dividing and dissipating the disciplines. In his examination of this theme as it is expressed in the Pentateuch and Historical Books, selected Prophets and Psalms, the author identifies and conserves the values to be gained by detailed correlation of sources of these composite works, and the distinctive formulations of the theme of retribution. Furthermore, he is able to trace a course of development or adaptation of this basic doctrine of biblical religion (it is also a constituent element of non-biblical religion) through the levels of literary composition from the United Monarchy to the end of the kingdom of Judah and the Babylonian Captivity.

The author is fully aware of the problems posed by the classic source analysis of the Pentateuch, including the chronology of literary composition and compilation, *i.e.,* JEDP roughly from the 10th through the 6th centuries B. C. As the extensive footnotes show, he is fully aware of the many corrections, alterations, adjustments, and refinements which have been proposed and promoted by unnumbered scholars in the intervening years. Following his own brisk course in rejecting many of the more popular proposals, accepting some, and modifying and qualifying others, he presents a persuasive argument for the classic chronology of literary composition and he develops this argument from a novel perspective: a comparative analysis of the wilderness historiographies of JE and all the subsequent sources.

He then tracks the theme of divine retribution through these sources chronologically. Not surprisingly, but contrary to certain cherished opinions, the theme is an essential ingredient in *all* of the sources, and the primal elements remain constant throughout. J and E have commonly been regarded mainly as narrative sources, lacking a coherent and comprehensive theology. But the author challenges that widespread view, demonstrating that JE does contain a systematic theology in the form of a consistent system of divine retribution. Moreover, the retributive theology of JE renders conditional the unconditional Promise to the Patriarchs of the land. Pursuant to this conclusion, he argues that the JE theology is the source of the subsequent Deuteronomic theology, not only of the latter's structure but also of its characteristic intensity. That God, the God of the Fathers and of Israel, is just and consistent in meting out rewards and punishments, is a truism, but there are many variations on this theme, and nuances in formulation and application which reflect sensitivities and accommodations to different times and circumstances. Adamiak rightly emphasizes the universality and continuity of the principle in general terms against those who, on dogmatic grounds, hold a different and in my opinion highly questionable position, radically bifurcating grace and law, mercy and judgment, as though these were separable entities in the biblical message. Equally impressive is his presentation of the alterations and modifications in the basic thesis of divine retribution as he follows the different sources through the Torah and Former Prophets.

Both the method and the results can be tested by looking at two matters of serious theological import with which the various authors and editors have to cope. They are quite familiar and traditional problems, but receive creative treatment at the hands of the author.

1) *The issue of the forty-year Wandering or the Generation Gap in the Wilderness.* The tradition of a forty-year Wandering or Sojourn in the Wilderness is deeply embedded in the sources, though perhaps not part of the original story. That datum is linked to the affirmation that the new generation departed from Egypt and died in the Wilderness, and was succeeded by the generation which en-

tered and took possession of the Promised Land. There are other statements, which affirm with equal clarity, that it was the same generation which went out of Egypt with Moses that also entered the land of Canaan with Joshua (Deuteronomy apparently attests both traditions in adjoining passages). According to Adamiak the conflicting assertions can be sorted out and assigned to different editors (*e.g.,* Dt and Dtr). More to the point, the author shows that the difference in viewpoint is rooted in divergent theological perceptions: For JE (for example), the remnant of the same group which rebelled in the Wilderness could nevertheless occupy the Promised Land as the beneficiary of the divine commitment to the Patriarchs, while for Dtr and P such a combination was unthinkable. Those who sinned, and remained unrepentant, had to be punished, not rewarded. They could not inherit the land, so a new innocent generation had to arise for that purpose. A persuasive correlation between the theological insights and the historical circumstances in which the different accounts of the Wilderness experience were written is developed: JE during the First Temple period when at least part of the Promised Land remained in Israelite or Judahite hands; Dtr and P during the Exile, after the final loss of the land. There is a necessary consistency in the theological interpretation of both periods: the Wilderness on the one hand, and the period of the Monarchy or the Exile on the other. God must be seen as meting out the same kind of justice under all conditions, but especially in the normative circumstances of the Exodus-Wanderings-Settlement, and in those contemporary with the author. The immediately visible circumstances in which the author or editor lives reflect divine decisions and actions, and the same pattern is perceived or imposed on the conditions of the earlier times. At the same time, the received record of the past conditions the interpretation of both past and present and thus determines to some degree its own revision.

2) *The problem of the individual and the community.* While in the main, the theme of divine retribution is concerned with the community and deals in historical events which express divine intervention as Judge and Savior, there is nevertheless a pervasive interest in the experience and fate of the individual. In the primary narrative, the fate of Israel is the prime consideration, and the question of divine justice is debated in reference to the experience of the people as a whole. According to Adamiak, in the older sources, the punishments inflicted in the Wilderness need not be exhaustive, or even distinguish carefully between guilty and innocent;

hence, guilty survivors can share in subsequent blessings, and even possess the Promised Land. At the same time, the fate of the individual was too important to be ignored or subsumed in the destiny of the nation, and the conflict, potential or real, between the many and the one, was already inherent in the covenant patterns from the start.

Certainly in the later sources, the question of the individual received major attention, and with the prophets of the 7th-6th centuries, the autonomy of each person in the divine scheme of retribution is emphasized, especially in Ezekiel who puts it so radically that the role of the community has been reduced to insignificance. Everyone will receive from God exactly what he or she deserves; there are no transfers, no continuity from one generation to another; each person is a discrete entity, entirely independent of all others. The reflex of this drastic departure from tradition is precisely the contention that the generation which rebelled against God in the Wilderness had to perish in the Wilderness, and only an entirely innocent generation could enter and inherit the land. That view expresses in collective terms the attitude of the exilic writers who saw in the destruction of Judah and the Babylonian Captivity the judgment of God against an equally rebellious and punishable generation. Provision, nevertheless, had to be made for the exceptional persons who maintained steadfastly their righteousness even in the midst of rebellion and destruction: the Exiles (who are characterized as the Good Figs by Jeremiah, and similarly by Ezekiel, even though the latter is more critical of his fellow-captives), and in the earlier period, Joshua and Caleb and their families.

The author has demonstrated the value of traditional higher criticism in conjunction with serious theological inquiry into the biblical text. He has defended the validity of the basic source analysis of the Primary History, and gone on from there to show its importance in tracing the divergent views of the doctrine of divine retribution in the literary materials. The source analysis provides the basis for the isolation of the theological threads, while the discussion of the latter offers clarification and refinement of the former. In conclusion, the reconstruction and presentation of the central theological theme and variations shed light on and offer support for the critical analysis of the sources.

David Noel Freedman

University of Michigan, Ann Arbor
1981

Preface

This monograph is a comparative study of the successive Old Testament historiographies of the wilderness generation, *i. e.,* that contingent which was delivered from Egypt and travelled through the Wilderness to the Promised Land. The study has several interrelated objectives, historical and theoretical. Historically, it analyzes the accounts of that generation contained in the following sources: the Jahwist (J) of the tenth century; the Elohist (E) of the ninth or eighth centuries; pre-exilic Prophecy; Deuteronomy (D) and the earlier edition of the Deuteronomic (Dt) history; the latter Deuteronomistic redaction (Dtr) of that history; the Priestly writing (P); exilic Prophecy and the relevant Psalms of various dates.[1] The identities and dates of these sources are provisional and the reasons for their acceptance, rejection or modification are provided in the course of the study. This study begins with J; no attempt is made to trace the pre-literary evolution of the wilderness itinerary or its

---

[1] The following may be conveniently and profitably consulted: Norman Habel, *Literary Criticism of the Old Testament* (Philadelphia: Fortress Press, 1971); Ronald E. Clements, *A Century of Old Testament Study* (London: Lutterworth, 1976); Klaus Koch, *The Growth of the Biblical Tradition: The Form-Critical Method* (London: Black, 1969); G. W. Andersen, *Tradition and Interpretation* (Oxford: Clarendon Press, 1979).

murmuring motif, although relevant opinions concerning these are provided.

On the basis of individual source analysis, conclusions are offered as to content and character, the continuities and variations among the successive sources, and the successive interactions of the historiographies. The study is in one sense a systematic analysis of the interaction of faith and history: faith expressed in history and subsequent history conditioned by that faith which it both sustains and modifies. This is the approach advocated several decades ago by Artur Weiser:

> Without the fact of a reciprocal interaction between faith and history the solution of the underlying theological problems lacks a firm foundation. *Old Testament faith is only intelligible when one is aware of the influence which history has had on the formation of this faith and, on the other hand, Old Testament history can only be understood from the point where faith as a historiographical force is recognized and taken into account.*[2]

Because of the perspicuity of the continuities and modifications in the wilderness historiographies, they afford an especially auspicious occasion to observe those features of Old Testament historiography which their interactions exemplify.

Theoretically, the study analyzes the wilderness historiographies and their interactions, *vis-à-vis* the character of Old Testament historiography, especially regarding the inveterate problem of the distinction between myth and history, where the former is construed as an explanation for cyclical and thus essentially atemporal events, and the latter denotes a linear sequence of non-repeatable, unique

[2] Arthur Weiser, "Glaube und Geschichte im Alten Testament" (1931), reprinted in his *Glaube und Geschichte im Alten Testament und andere ausgewählte Schriften* (Göttingen: Vandenhoeck und Ruprecht, 1961), p. 100; for a similar view see the remarks of O. Cullman, *Salvation in History* (New York: Harper and Row, 1967), p. 88: "Each new event recognized in faith as belonging to salvation history is linked in its verticality with earlier interpretations of earlier events by the Old Testament writers. In this way light is thrown from the earlier events upon the new, but likewise a totally new light is thrown from the new upon the old.... Each time *corrections* of the interpretation of past saving events *are undertaken in the light of the new events.* This, of course, never happens in such a way that an earlier account is disputed"; and Rudolf Smend, "Tradition and History: A Complex Relation," in Douglas Knight, ed., *Tradition and Theology in the Old Testament* (Philadelphia: Fortress Press, 1977), p. 65.

events. In this regard the study addresses the problem stated by Marsh, namely, the "ontological status of history."[3] This study is somewhat anomalous because its own conception and execution also exemplify certain salient characteristics which it attempts to identify and analyze in the ancient Israelite historian-theologians. The study, which is an analysis of Old Testament conceptions of origins, the successive accounts of the origins of the settlement of the Promised Land, is itself a study of origins.

Focusing initially on Western eschatology in the nineteenth century, at the suggestion of Professor Edward Shils I extended the inquiry to include some of the earlier manifestations of that phenomenon. In the course of that extended inquiry it became clear that the Book of Daniel, commonly regarded as the first example of Old Testament apocalyptic eschatology, was itself the product of a long Israelite historiographic-theological tradition which had endeavored to establish the justice of history. This study is the product of my researches into those earlier traditions.

During these researches several problems presented themselves which appeared unresolved by Old Testament scholars. I undertook to examine these problems and took the liberty of sending the preliminary results of the inquiry to those scholars who might be especially interested in them—Professors David Noel Freedman and Volkmar Fritz. Both scholars, displaying a rare magnanimity and dedication to truth, responded to my inquiry with interest, criticism, numerous suggestions for the pursuit of the project, encouragement and offers of additional assistance. It is of interest to note that the suggestions of both were quite similar. Through several drafts, Professor Freedman has most generously and patiently shared with me his interest, experience and enthusiasm as well as his trenchant and sympathetic suggestions, both as a scholar and as an editor, despite his many other pressing committments. Professor Arnaldo Momigliano likewise generously offered several important observations and suggestions. This work is one of the results of a graduate seminar, "Tradition and Traditional Institutions," given several years ago by Professor Edward Shils, from which has emerged his recently published treatise entitled *Tradition* . For that seminal experience and for Professor Shils' continued interest, generosity and patience, I am profoundly grateful. For such merit as

---

[3] J. Marsh, *The Fullness of Time* (New York: Harper and Row, 1952), p. 13.

this work has, the efforts of these scholars are largely responsible; the sole responsibility for its failings lies with the author.

Ann Grimes undertook a taxing editorial task and managed to turn the text into an intelligible exposition. Mrs. Charmian Kühr of the Kress Library of the Lutheran School of Theology was most helpful throughout in securing the necessary materials.

Richard Adamiak

Chicago
September, 1981

TABLE OF CONTENTS

Introduction

This work offers a series of interrelated hypotheses concerning the historiographies of the wilderness generation contained in the successive sources. The prevailing opinions regarding these sources and their historiographies are examined in the relevant sections of the work. The hypotheses are:

1) Contrary to the inveterate view, JE does contain a systematic and consistent theology in the form of a consistent system of divine retribution. If retributive theology is construed to be a consistent normative system, ascribed to a divinity, enjoining some actions and prohibiting others, with a consistent corresponding system of rewards and punishments, then such a system is demonstrably present in JE, almost as much in evidence there as in the later Deuteronomic theology. It is neither as dramatic nor as severe as those of the subsequent sources but with regard to the Wilderness, it is as consistent and as comprehensive in its theological interpretation of the phenomena it records.

2) The JE theology is a covenant theology, based on the Sinaitic covenant, which renders the unconditional Promise to the Patriarchs of the land conditional.

3) Due to the collective character of JE's system of retribution,

according to which the divine punishment of some of the people is a
symbolic punishment of all of them, those who reach the Promised
Land are not the innocent remnant, but rather those who were not
lethally punished for their sins in the Wilderness. JE portrays the
Wilderness generation as unfaithful.

4) Until now we have been speaking of JE, but a cogent argument may be made for J alone. Here the problem is not one of significant differences between the J and E wilderness historiographies but rather the identification of elements and their assignment
to either of the sources. This procedure is notoriously difficult in
the Sinai pericope whose contents are still much disputed.[4] The
analysis of J as a separate source, based on the consensus of recent
scholarship, affords the opportunity to discuss J as a theologian.

5) The pre-exilic Prophets and pre-exilic Psalter differ radically
from JE in their portrayals of the wilderness period. They view it as
a period of idyllic faithfulness and divine favor. Although the explicit reliance of these sources on the covenant is problematic, the
pre-exilic prophets clearly regard the nation as obligated to God for
His miraculous past actions on its behalf, which they embellish;
and they threaten punishments for violations of the divine law. The
retributive system in those sources resembles that of JE; it is a collective system in which the entire nation is threatened with punishment for the evil actions of some of its members, although there are
exceptions.

6) The JE covenant theology, expressed in its wilderness historiography, is the source of both the structure and contents of the later Deuteronomic theology; it is also the source of the latter's char-

---

[4] Regarding Exod., The. Vriezen, in "The Exegesis of Exodus XXIV, 9-11," *The
Witness of Tradition* (Papers read at the Joint British-Dutch Old Testament Conference Held at Woudschoten, 1970; Leiden: Brill, 1972), p. 100, has written that "the
Jahwistic and Elohistic sources were intermingled to such an extent that it is — in
many respects — impossible to separate them and to trace the sources any further
than the Jehovistic work JE." In the view of M. Noth, *A History of the Pentateuchal Traditions* (New Jersey: Prentice, 1972, pp. 32n-33n), a somewhat similar diffi-
culty obtains in the second half of Num., where several murmuring incidents occur,
due to "a variety of additions made in various literary stages, as well as . . . the far-
reaching results of the literary combination of the Pentateuch with the Deuteronomistic history." The same author, M. Noth, asserts in *Numbers: A Commentary*
(Philadelphia: Westminster, 1968), p. 149, that the first instance in Num. which can
definitely be attributed to E occurs in Chapter 20; in the opinion of G. W. Coats, in
*Rebellion in the Wilderness: The Murmuring Motif in the Wilderness Tradition of
the Old Testament* (Nashville: Abington, 1968), p. 194, "the murmuring never clearly appears in E."

acteristic intensity. The apparent confirmation of JE by subsequent religious and political events imparted to JE an overwhelming authority in the eyes of the Deuteronomic theologians.

7) Based on the clearly discernible difference in their wilderness historiographies, the existence of two editions of the Deuteronomic history may be inferred, one pre-exilic, the other exilic. The first of these, Dt, employs a system of individual retribution. The second, Dtr, reverts to the original concept of collective responsibility. Both changes were dictated by the course of events; if the pre-exilic nation was doomed because of the sins of the previous generations, then no degree of reform could avert destruction; after the exile the system of collective retribution was reasserted to explain the calamity—which had occurred despite such laudable events as Josiah's reforms.

8) The modifications in the wilderness historiographies of JE and Dt effected by Dtr are reflected in exilic Prophecy, the exilic Psalms, and in P.

9) Only in Ezekiel does the individual clearly emerge as a moral entity completely separate from the nation. With the loss of all the land, theretofore the visible evidence for divine reward and punishment, the individual stands alone, answerable to God for his actions, and subject to the rewards and punishments which those actions incur. Many explanations have been offered for the origin of apocalyptic eschatology in the Old Testament. In the course of this study, salient factors relevant to that origin have emerged which have been neglected: a) The attempt to find justice in the visible world (and in its record) by the consistent unification of the moral and the ontological, which is what apocalyptic eschatology essentially represents, is not attributable to this or that particular fact, but rather it emerges from the earlier Old Testament historiographical traditions which had addressed the same problem; b) The loss of the Promised Land, the visible manifestation of divine reward and punishment of the nation as a collective moral entity, coupled with the simultaneous disintegration of that collective entity and concomitant emergence of the individual moral entity, shifted the examination of the whole problem of justice in history to a different plane. All the foregoing factors rendered the Old Testament religion particularly receptive to the individual and transcendental eschatology of Zoroastrianism with which the Israelites came into contact at about this time, *i.e.*, during the Exile.

10) Theoretically, it is the innate propensity for intelligibility within a context of evolving events, which is the entelechy of the process to which this monograph addresses itself. The wilderness period is an archetype. It portrays in didactic-paradigmatic form that which occurred in the constitutive phase of the covenantally expressed interrelation of God and Israel.[5] Although an archetype, it is not immutable but rather is subject to modifications which are determined by its interaction with the phenomena which constitute the configuration of subsequent relevant events, events whose interpretation it simultaneously conditions. The sequence under consideration here is a linear sequence of non-repeatable events, which, although unique, are rendered intelligible only by their inclusion within a consistent historical configuration whose consistency and apparent immutability are expressed and thus explained in an archetype. While this archetype is mythic, in that it represents an apparently eternally valid explanation for each phase of the evolving configuration, its reliability as an authoritative source requires occasional modification from phase to phase to harmonize emerging inconsistencies, between its portrayal-explanation on the one hand, and the phenomena of its evolving configuration on the other. The modifications may be more evident during formative phases, but the process which the modifications exemplify is universal. The Old Testament wilderness historiography is a particularly dramatic and thus visible example of this universal process. All explanatory historiography is necessarily theoretical because all explanations are necessarily theoretical and archetypes are a particular form of theoretical explanation.

---

[5] A. Tunyogi, in *The Rebellion of Israel* (Richmond: John Knox Press, 1969), pp. 92-95, has called attention to the archetypical nature of the wilderness experience, but by attributing to one source, "the Tetrateuchal author," elements from widely different periods, he places incorrect emphasis on the static nature of the archetype as a whole, ignoring its dynamism which is revealed by its successive modifications; in contrast: I. Engnell, in *A Rigid Scrutiny: Critical Essays in the Old Testament* (Nashville: Abington Press, 1969), p. 214, regards the wilderness as a non-repeatable event and, ignoring the murmuring motif, concludes that "it seems wholly unlikely that a forty-year wandering through the wilderness . . . involving such difficult external circumstances and great hardships . . . would have created and leavened Israel's entire manner of life and future ideal"; this also obscures the fact that the hazards of the wilderness, which are magnified in pre-exilic prophecy, have the effect of enhancing the miraculousness of the divine guidance through it, thus increasing the obligation of the nation to obey.

1: The Jahwist Wilderness Historiography

The question of the existence of a consistent retributive theology in JE is frequently ignored; when the question is broached it is usually denied. Although pre-exilic episodes such as the Primal Fall, the Deluge and the destruction of Sodom and Gomorrah are recognized as examples of a retributive theology, that theology is not traced into the pre-exilic history. For example, in the view of Gerhard von Rad: "The Deuteronomic historian decisively attributes to the kings the power to choose freely for or against Yahweh in contrast to the so-called classical historians of Israel, who rather depict humanity as the passive object of God's purpose in history."[6]

Elsewhere, when speaking of J and E, von Rad refers to the

[6] Gerhard von Rad, in "The Deuteronomic Theology of History in I and II Kings," *The Problem of the Hextateuch and Other Essays* (New York: McGraw-Hill, 1966), pp. 206-207; for similar views: G. Hölscher, *Geschichtsschreibung in Israel: Untersuchungen zum Jahwisten und Elohisten* (Lund: Gleerup, 1952), esp. pp. 119-131; S. Mowinckel, "Israelite Historiography," *Annual of the Swedish Theological Institute* (1963), p. 15; A. Alt, "Die Deutung der Weltgeschichte im Alten Testament," *Grundzüge der Geschichte des Volkes Israel* (München: Beck, 1967), p. 444; Samuel Amsler, "Les Deux Sources de le théologie de l'Histoire dans l'Ancien Testament," *Revue de Théologie et Philosophie*, 19 (1969), p. 254.

"preponderance of the matter-of-fact historical over the theological which is so characteristic of the witness of Israel" and reiterates his opinion that "Israel only finally went over to the prosaic and scientific presentations of her history with the Deuteronomic history."[7] It is the J and E understanding of history "that man can be saved only by the free action of God himself, not through some righteousness of their own by which they could preserve themselves and others from divine judgment."[8] Wolff dates the emergence of retributive history from Jeremiah.[9] Wolfhart Pannenberg is in agreement with von Rad: "Promise alone controls the course of history in the account of the succession to the throne and with the Yahwist . . . the D account, on the other hand, attaches a qualification to the promise—the qualification of the fulfillment of the law."[10] Moshe Weinfeld is of a similar opinion: "Deuteronomy and the deuteronomic school made both the grant of the land and the promise of dynasty conditional on observance of the law, in their view, the most dominant and fateful factor in the history of Israel."[11]

According to Cross, "In J there is not a hint of the prophetic covenant-lawsuit,"[12] and in the opinion of Speiser, in J's history "man is but an unwary tool in the hands of the Supreme Power who charts the course of the universe."[13] One of the closest students of Deuteronomic theology, Moshe Weinberg, shares this opinion:

> J and E are merely narrative sources in which no
> uniform outlook and concrete ideology can as yet

[7] von Rad, *Old Testament Theology* (2 vols., New York: Harper and Row, 1962-1965), I, pp. 109, 125; Smend, "Tradition and History," p. 67.

[8] von Rad, *Old Testament Theology,* I, pp. 106, 109, 112, 114-115, 128.

[9] Hans Walter Wolff, "The Kerygma of the Yahwist," in Walter Brueggemann and Hans Walter Wolff, eds., *The Vitality of Old Testament Traditions* (Atlanta: John Knox Press, 1975), pp. 59, 61-62.

[10] W. Pannenberg, "Redemptive Event and History," in Klaus Westermann, ed., *Essays in Old Testament Hermeneutics* (Richmond: John Knox Press, 1963), p. 318.

[11] M. Weinfeld, *Deuteronomy and the Deuteronomic School* (New York: Oxford University Press, 1971), p. 81.

[12] Frank M. Cross, *Canaanite Myth and Hebrew Epic* (Cambridge: Harvard, 1973), p. 264.

[13] E. A. Speiser, *Genesis: A Commentary* (AB; New York: Doubleday, 1964), p. xxvi.

be discerned and this contrasts strongly with P and deuteronomic literature, each of which embodies a complex and consistent theology which we may search for in vain in the earlier sources.[14]

On the other hand, the existence of a retributive theology in some of the episodes in J's pre-Egypt narrative is readily admitted by some. For example, Martin Noth writes that "the entire weight of the theology of J rests upon the beginning of his narrative." While he did add the *Urgeschichte*, the later materials he simply recorded as received: "It sufficed for him to have said plainly at the beginning how he intended to understand everything beyond that."[15] Stoebe, however, does go somewhat beyond this, calling attention to the similarities of the Primal Fall on the one hand and, on the other hand, the wilderness episodes in Exod. 14:12, Num. 11:18 and Num. 14:3,[16] but he does not explore this systematically.

Recently, several authorities have questioned the very existence of a J source as traditionally conceived, attributing those elements previously ascribed to J to Deuteronomic theologians of the seventh century or later.[17]

In contrast to the views of most authorities, the existence of a more systematic retributive theology in the earlier sources has been mentioned but not demonstrated. For example, David Noel Freedman has written that there is in biblical history a pattern of retributive theology based on covenants; a system of obedience resulting in blessings and disobedience resulting in punishment:

> In a general way the major historical work of the Bible, which traces the experience of Israel from the earliest times until the fall of Jerusalem and

---

[14] Weinfeld, *Deuteronomy*, p. 179.

[15] Noth, *Pentateuchal Traditions*, p. 239; for a similar view see Lothar Ruppert, "Der Jahwist — Künder der Heilsgeschichte," in Josef Schreiner, ed., *Wort und Botschaft: Eine Theologische und Kritische Einführung in die Probleme des Alten Testaments* (Würzburg: Echter, 1967), p. 105.

[16] H. J. Stoebe, "Gut und Böse in der Jahwistischen Quelle des Pentateuch," *ZAW* 65 (1954), p. 204.

[17] Rolf Rendtorff, *Die Überlieferungsgeschichtlichen Probleme des Pentateuchs, BZAW* 147 (Berlin: de Gruyter, 1977), pp. 73-79, 108, 112, 158, 163-164; Hans Heinrich Schmid, *Der Sogenannte Jahwist* (Zürich: Theologischer Verlag, 1976), *passim;* for discussions of these views see: *Journal for the Study of the Old Testament* 3 (July, 1977), pp. 2-60.

the exile of Judah (*i.e.,* the Primary History: Genesis—Kings) follows this pattern and attempts an
interpretation of the data in terms of covenant
making and breaking, renewal and rejection.[18]

But more recently the same author has stated that "the king is
always thought of as subordinate to the covenant; in this respect,
DTR's theology contrasts with the more ambiguous view of JE and
early monarchic poetry."[19]

A recent view, however, which agrees with Freedman's earlier
opinion is that of Hannelis Schulte, who concludes that "Justice is
the persistent theme from the stories of Genesis to the books of
Samuel."[20] This view, however, virtually ignores the Wilderness
and covenant theology. A somewhat similar and more precise conclusion is presented by Zenger:

> ... The ambivalence of human life, according to
> which man wants to take control of his life and
> precisely in doing so forfeits the power over his
> life, is portrayed by the Jahwist for his contempo-
> raries not only in the primordial history and the
> individual fates of the patriarchal period, but also
> in the "popular history" of the exodus-wilderness
> and acquisition epoch. The arrogant willfulness of
> man is according to the Jahwist a denial of Jah-
> weh.[21]

Although offering a conclusion with regard to the Wilderness, Zenger does not treat that period systematically and, while his conclusion is acceptable, it remains to be compared with those works
which do explore the wilderness historiography of J and E. With
one exception these studies have concluded that J and E do not contain a consistent system of retribution. The most probable reason
for the denial of a consistent theology in J is the apparent inconsistency in its record of divine rewards and punishments. In some
places, certain actions are rewarded while in other places these

[18] David Noel Freedman, "The Biblical Idea of History," *Interpretation* 21
(1967), pp. 38-39.

[19] David Noel Freedman, "The Deuteronomic History," *IDB Supp.,* p. 227.

[20] H. Schulte, *Die Entstehung der Geschichtsschreibung im Alten Israel, BZAW*
128 (1972), p. 94.

[21] E. Zenger, *Die Sinaitheophanie: Untersuchungen zum jahwistischen und elohistischen Geschichtswerk, Forschung zur Bibel* 3 (Würzburg: Echter, 1971), pp.
144-145.

same actions seem to be punished. Intimately related to this view is the "murmuring motif," the expression of disobedience, which figures so prominently in the Jahwist account of the Wilderness. It is on this point that the question of a consistent retributive theology in J's wilderness historiography turns. George Coats, on the basis of his exhaustive analysis of the murmuring episodes, concludes that "even though punishment is apparently not foreign to the tradition, it has never played a decisive role." He attributes "the incongruous picture of Jahweh alternating between aid and punishment" to the fact that these different responses represent two separate themes in the wilderness tradition.[22] He regards as inconsistent the fact that while the murmuring episode in Exod. 16 is not punished, the parallel episode in Num. 11:4-34 is.[23] Martin Noth offers a similar view, noting in connection with the murmuring episode in Num. 21:4-9 that "the discontent of the people with the frugal life of the desert no longer leads, at the end of the period of the wilderness wanderings, as it has mostly done till now, to an act of divine help, but to an act of punishment of the discontented people who have risen against God and Moses."[24] Accordingly, there is no consistent pattern of retribution. If the student overlooks the decisive significance of the Sinaitic covenant in J's system of retribution, then the erratic and unpredictable divine responses to the acts of disobedience seem rather to constitute a system of divine terror. Such a system might of course be counted a theology, but it would leave the problem of good and evil as inscrutable as before.

On the other hand, Tunyogi does see a pattern in the rebellion episodes: "The stories have two main themes: the rebellions of humans and the grace of the Lord."[25] But this conclusion in unacceptable. Of those authorities who have addressed themselves to the

---

[22] Coats, *Rebellion in the Wilderness,* pp. 16, 38, 93, 94, 107-115, 149; his thesis is accepted by Walter Brueggemann, *The Land: Place as Gift, Promise and Challenge in Biblical Faith* (Philadelphia: Fortress, 1977), pp. 28, 35.

[23] Coats, *Rebellion,* pp. 107-114; and compare: Pierre Buis, "Les Conflicts entre Moise et Israel dans Exode et Nombres," *VT* 28 (1978), pp. 258-261; Schmid, *Der Sogenannte Jahwist,* pp. 64-78.

[24] Noth, *Numbers, OTL* (Philadelphia: Westminster, 1968), p. 157; in connection with the murmuring episode in Exod. 16, Brevard S. Childs, in *The Book of Exodus: A Critical, Theological Commentary, OTL,* (Philadelphia: Westminster, 1974), p. 282, notes that "the murmuring stems from rebellion against God (vv., 6ff.), but God is gracious in spite of unbelief"; he does not explain this graciousness.

[25] Tunyogi, *Rebellions of Israel,* pp. 34, 54.

Wilderness closely and systematically, only Volkmar Fritz has
clearly suggested a consistent retributive theology for this period in
the early historiography, and the seminal place of the Sinaitic covenant in that theology.[26]

Other relevant works are noted in the course of this study, especially those dealing with Deuteronomic wilderness historiography.
For the moment it is sufficient to note that Barth, von Rad, Childs
and Schmid contend that the wilderness generation is portrayed in
an increasingly negative light in Prophecy, history and the Psalter.[27] Von Rad and Weinfeld suggest that a connection exists between those portrayals and the deteriorating political circumstances
within which they were written.[28] But von Rad and Barth focus almost exclusively on the Psalms and Prophecy and neither they nor
Weinfeld offer an explanation for the relation between the historiographies and their circumstances. Moreover, as noted, both Weinfeld and von Rad deny a consistent theology of retribution to J and
E.

We now turn to the Jahwist account of the Wilderness. According to J in Exod. 2: "In the course of these many days the king of
Egypt died. And the people of Israel groaned under their bondage
and cried out for help, and their cry under bondage came up to
God. And God heard their groaning, and God remembered his covenant with Abraham, with Isaac, and with Jacob."[29] God responds
and here ensues the sequence of great signs and wonders culminat-
ing in their deliverance. The Israelites, camped at the shore of the
Red Sea and pursued by the Egyptians because of Pharaoh's
change of heart, are in great fear:

> And the people of Israel cried out to the Lord;
> and they said to Moses, "Is it because there are no
> graves in Egypt that you have taken us away to die
> in the wilderness? What have you done to us in
> bringing us out of Egypt? Is not this what we said

[26] Volkmar Fritz, *Israel in der Wüste: Traditionsgeschichtliche Untersuchungen der Wüstenüberlieferungen des Jahwisten, MTS* 7 (Marburg: Elwert, 1970), pp. 67-70.

[27] K. Barth, *"Zur Bedeutung der Wüstentradition," VT Supp.* 15 (1966), pp. 14-23; von Rad, *Old Testament Theology I*, pp. 280-285; Childs, *Exodus,* pp. 259-262; Schmid, *Der Sogenannte Jahwist,* pp. 80-81.

[28] von Rad, *Old Testament Theology,* I, pp. 280-285; Weinfeld, *Deuteronomy,* p. 31.

[29] Exod. 2:23-25 (All references are to the Revised Standard Version).

to you in Egypt, 'Let us alone and let us serve the
Egyptians'? For it would have been better for us
to serve the Egyptians than to die in the wilderness."[30]

Moses implores the people to be patient, and the great miracle at
the sea occurs, delivering the nation. J concludes the Exodus sequence as follows:

> Thus the Lord saved Israel that day from the
> hand of the Egyptians; and Israel saw the Egyp-
> tians dead upon the seashore. And Israel saw the
> great work which the Lord did against the Egyp-
> tians and the people feared the Lord and they be-
> lieved in the Lord and in his servant Moses.[31]

The fact that the great saving acts are expressly recorded as
"seen," *i.e.,* witnessed, is of critical importance in J and in later
wilderness historiographies, especially as this "seeing" is related to
the covenant.[32]

The next murmuring episode occurs at the wilderness of Shur, almost immediately after the climactic deliverance at the Red Sea, the
last of the great saving acts. The water at Marah was too bitter to
drink and "the people murmured against Moses, saying, 'What
shall we drink?' and he cried out to the Lord and the Lord showed
him a tree, and he threw it into the water, and the water became
sweet."[33] J sets this faithlessness in the sharpest relief: After having
seen all the great saving acts, the people's faith is shaken by the
mere bitterness of the water, a trifle in light of the great signs and
wonders and the miracle at the Red Sea just three days before. Still
there is no punishment for this faithlessness; the Lord provides
water.

---

[30] Exod. 14:10-12; these passages are commonly regarded as J; Coats, *Rebellion,*
181; B. S. Childs, *Exodus,* 220; but compare Noth, *Exodus: A Commentary, OTL*
(Philadelphia: Westminster, 1962), p. 112.

[31] *Ibid.,* 14:30-31; for the Exodus tradition in later Old Testament historiography
see: P. Weimar, *Geschichten und Geschichte der Befreiung Israels* (Stuttgart: KBW,
1975), p. 139.

[32] J. N. M. Wijngaards, "The Dramatization of Salvific History in the Deutero-
nomic Schools," *Oudtestamentische Studien* XVI (Leiden: Brill, 1969), pp. 43-49; I.
L. Seeligmann, "Erkenntnis Gottes und historisches Bewusstsein im alten Israel," in
Herbert Donner, ed., *Beiträge zur alttestamentlichen Theologie: Festschrift für
Walther Zimmerli zum 70. Geburtstag* (Göttingen: Vandenhoek und Ruprecht,
1977), pp. 434-435, 445.

[33] Exod. 15:24-25a.

The second episode occurs soon after, in the Wilderness of Sin. Here the original J murmuring event is phased out by P who replaces it with his own version.[34] It is clear from the response described in P that a lack of food caused the people to complain. As in the first episode there is no punishment. The divine response is the miraculous bestowal of manna.[35] But here a qualification is added by God; the manna is not given only as response to the murmuring, but "that I may prove them."[36] The Lord gives instructions as to how much manna is to be gathered daily and orders that a double portion be gathered each sixth day.[37] From the continuation of the J account in Exod. 16:29-30, it is clear that either or both of these strictures were violated by some, requiring Moses to censure the people and warn them again to rest on the seventh day, the Sabbath. This they finally do.[38] Here, outright disobedience instead of faithlessness is dramatized but no punishment ensues. The Jahwist concludes that the people ate the manna, "till they came to the border of the land of Canaan."[39]

The next murmuring episode, recounted in Exod. 17, occurs in the wilderness at Meriba. The people "found fault with Moses" because there was no water to drink.[40] This complaint surpasses mere murmuring for now the people nearly stone Moses.[41] Still there is no punishment. The Lord instructs Moses to strike the rock and water bursts forth, "in the sight of the elders of Israel" who witness the miracle.[42] Fritz rightly observes that this episode represents an intensification of the murmuring motif: "The failing of the people is no longer merely an understandable reaction to the need for

[34] M. Noth, *Exodus*, pp. 133-134; for similar views see B. S. Childs, *Exodus*, pp. 279-280; Fritz, *Israel*, pp. 9, 42; on the other hand, Coats (*Rebellion*, pp. 94-95) asserts that a J complaint did not necessarily exist here; for fuller details see Noth, *Pentateuchal Traditions*, pp. 122-123.

[35] Exod. 16:4-5a.

[36] Exod. 16:4bb.

[37] *Ibid.*, 16:4-5

[38] *Ibid.*, 16:29-30.

[39] *Ibid.*, 16:35b.

[40] *Ibid.*, 17:2.

[41] *Ibid.*, 17:4-5.

[42] *Ibid.*, 17:6; cf. Coats, *Rebellion*, pp. 61-62.

water during the wandering, but is conceived as a lack of faith."[43] Despite the intensification, the episode is followed immediately by the Israelite victory over Amalek, achieved by divine assistance.[44] To this point there have been four episodes of murmuring: None is punished, and all are followed by still more miraculous acts.

[43] Fritz, *Israel,* p. 53; Noth (*Exodus,* p. 139) ascribes 17:3 to E, the remainder, except for the introduction and minor insertions, to J; but Childs (*Exodus,* p. 306) asserts that the content of Ex. 17:1-7 "cannot be decided with any degree of certainty." Coats (*Rebellion,* p. 70) with a few exceptions with which we are not here concerned, ascribes the murmuring incident and its result to J.

[44] Exod. 17:8-13; this episode, with the exception of v. 14, while it has been attributed to E, nevertheless appears to derive from J originally; cf. Fritz, *Israel,* pp. 12-13; Noth, *Exodus,* p. 141; Noth, *Pentateuchal Traditions,* p. 119; Childs (*Exodus,* p. 313) states that the basic Amalek story "gives the impression of being ancient."

2: The Sinaitic Covenant

The existence of a covenant made at Sinai, recorded by either J or E, or both, has been affirmed, questioned and emphatically denied.[45] More of certainty can be said concerning the question of a covenant in J by an analysis of those murmuring episodes which occur before and after Sinai. But the apostasy at Sinai merits consideration.

It is agreed among scholars that the J cultic decalogue in Exod. 34 has been displaced from its original position earlier in the sequence, before the apostasy recounted in Exod. 32-33.[46] When the J

[45] Cf.: Noth, *Pentateuchal Traditions,* pp. 141, 153; von Rad, *Problem of the Hextateuch,* p. 53; W. Beyerlin, *Origins of the Oldest Sinaitic Traditions* (Oxford: Blackwell's, 1961), pp. 33-34, 51-57; Zenger, *Sinaitheophanie,* p. 147; Hartmut Gese, "Bemerkungen zur Sinaitradition," *ZAW* 79 (1967), p. 145; Walther Zimmerli, *The Law and the Prophets* (Oxford: Blackwell's, 1965), p. 31; E. W. Nicholson, *Exodus and Sinai in History and Tradition* (Richmond: John Knox Press, 1973), pp. 74, 76; D. J. McCarthy, *Old Testament Covenant: A Survey of Current Opinion* (Richmond: John Knox Press, 1972), p. 57; Lothar Perlitt, *Bundestheologie im Alten Testament,* WMANT 36 (Neukirchen-Vluyn: Neukirchner Verlag, 1969), pp. 156-238; Th. C. Vriezen, "The Exegesis of Exodus XXIV: 9-11," in *The Witness of Tradition,* pp. 100-133, esp. 117n.

[46] Noth, *Exodus,* pp. 260-261; Zenger, *Sinaitheophanie,* p. 122; Beyerlin, *Origins,* p. 81; Childs, *Exodus,* p. 608; Roland de Vaux, *The Early History of Israel,*

decalogue was moved to its present position the theme of the broken tables was added to render the modification consistent with the preceding material.[47] Thus the apostasy originally followed the J decalogue and its other elements.

The apostasy of the calf in its present literary form is usually attributed to E, but most authorities share the view that it is an expanded version of an earlier similar episode recounted by J.[48]

Irrespective of the exact content of the original J account in Exod. 32-33, one may ascertain that, regarding its retributive structure, the punishment of the plague in v. 35 follows some act of disobedience in J.[49] Noth is of the view that the plague punishment in the J account immediately followed the apostasy.[50] He also suggests that it might constitute the continuation and conclusion of the punishment represented by the "water of cursing" whose consequences are not given.[51] Because of the fragmentary nature of J here, and the unknown result of the plague, the details of J's system of retribution exemplified in this episode remain problematic. Nevertheless, the structure of that system of retribution may be inferred, revealing the obligation of the nation to obey or face punishment for disobedience. This contrasts sharply with the pre-Sinaitic murmuring incidents which went unpunished. It may be argued that the magnitude of the sin at Sinai accounts for the different divine responses but an examination of subsequent murmuring episodes will eliminate consideration for this possibility.

(Philadelphia: Westminster, 1978), pp. 398-402, 444-447; if the covenant is very narrowly conceived, its character and similarity to the vassal treaties may be disputed; seen in broader perspective, however, *i.e.,* as an element in J's historiography, its place in that scheme, and its character, are quite clear; the people were "witnesses" to each of the deeds which precede the events of Sinai; does this witnessing have no purpose?

[47] Beyerlin, *Origins,* v. 77; M. Noth, *Exodus,* p. 260; Otto Eissfeldt, *The Old Testament: An Introduction* (New York: Harper and Row, 1965), p. 215; Childs, *Exodus,* p. 608.

[48] Cf. Noth, *Exodus,* pp. 245-246; Coats, *Rebellion,* p. 188; Childs, *Exodus,* pp. 558-560; the latter opines that the J account may even have contained a calf; Beyerlin *(Origins)* attributes it in its original form to E.

[49] Childs, *Exodus,* p. 558; Coats, *Rebellion,* p. 188.

[50] Noth, *Exodus,* p. 252.

[51] Noth, *Exodus,* pp. 243, 251; but Childs *(Exodus,* p. 559), believes that to interpret the curse water as a punishment is to overinterpret the symbolism; his view that a punishment would stand in tension with the larger framework of the chapter is questionable; the curse accords with them perfectly.

Having displaced the original J cultic decalogue covenant with its own, the E account of the Golden Calf is the first episode to occur after the covenant. Its version of apostasy and punishment compounds the original J punishment by breaking the tablets and thereby abrogating the covenant. By doing so it sustains the structure of J's system of retribution. In the episode the people lose faith when Moses ("this man who brought us up out of the land of Egypt"[52]) delays returning from the mountain. Aaron orders the people to bring their gold to him and "he fashioned it with a graving tool and made a molten calf."[53] He builds an altar before it and proclaims it the Lord. The people sacrifice to it and celebrate.[54] Moses returns infuriated and destroys the calf.[55] Aaron's duplicity is so characteristic of J's relentless irony that it is difficult to ascribe it to another source.[56]

In the vv. 30-34 Moses offers to make atonement for the people's sin. Although the plague punishment in v. 35 is retained from the earlier account, in vv. 30-35, in response to Moses' efforts, the Lord says, "Whoever has sinned against me, him I will blot out of my book . . . in the day when I visit I will visit their sin upon them.[57] Retaining the older punishment, this part, which is a supplement to J, or E, while it defers punishment, still asserts the principle of liability to punishment. By the same token the principle of individual responsibility seems to be asserted, though this is problematic since the J account of the sin, used as a basis for the E expansion, gives the impression that the entire nation participated in the apostasy. Yet the passage states that only the guilty will be punished when the punishment is inflicted. The E form of the decalogue makes no clear assertion concerning liability since Exod. 20:5-6, which speaks of the liability of later generations for the evil deeds of earlier generations, is a Deuteronomic addition.[58]

[52] Exod. 32:1-2.

[53] *Ibid.,* 32:4-6.

[54] *Ibid.,* 32:4-6

[55] *Ibid.,* 32:22-24.

[56] When Adam and Eve are confronted by the Lord with their sin, Adam avoids responsibility by imputing the sin to "the woman whom thou gavest to be with me, she gave me the fruit of the tree and I ate," Eve's defense is "the serpent beguiled me and I ate"; *Gen.,* 3:12-13.

[57] Exod. 32:33-34.

[58] Noth, *Exodus,* p. 163; Weinfeld, *Deuteronomy,* pp. 81, 317.

3: J's Wilderness Historiography Continued

Three days after the departure from Sinai the J account resumes in Num. 11:

> And the people complained in the hearing of the Lord about their misfortunes; and when the Lord heard it his anger was kindled, and the fire of the Lord burned among them, and consumed some outlying parts of the camp. Then the people cried out to Moses; and Moses prayed to the Lord and the fire abated. So the name of the place was called Tabera, because the fire of the Lord burned among them.[59]

Here we have an episode which is attributed by all to J. In contrast to the Golden Calf incident of Exod. 32-33, it is free from the superimposition of subsequent elements. While the original J content of Exod. 32-33 may be somewhat problematic, this episode is unambiguous and lucidly reveals the seminal importance of the covenant in J's theology of retribution. In the words of Volkmar Fritz:

> In contrast to the episode of the bitter water in

[59] Num., 11:1-3; cf. Noth, *Numbers,* p. 83; Coats, *Rebellion,* pp. 124-125; Fritz (*Israel,* p. 69) offers an explanation for the use of "camp."

Mara, Exod. 15:22-25a, and the spring miracle in
Meriba, Exod. 17:1bB, 2, 4-7, in the story of the
fire in Tabera Israel is not involved in a natural
need but rather the people have merited the catastrophe by their own behavior. The exposition of
this episode reveals a decisive change in contrast
to the previous wilderness episodes. The people
do not rebel against Moses because of a need, as
in Exod. 15:24 and 17:2, but rather the threat to
the camp and its inhabitants is a consequence of a
rebellion which is directed against Jahweh. Hence
the fire is not an accidental natural phenomenon,
but the divine punishment for the improper behavior of the people . . . the fire in the camp at
Tabera portrays the first event after the departure
from Sinai. With Num. 10: 33a and 11:1-3, the
Jahwist has begun to portray the second part of
the wilderness wandering under the aspect of disobedience and apostasy. The behavior of the people is clearly negatively qualified. Because of its
complaints and murmuring Israel provokes Jahweh's wrath, even if he does not deny the people
his help to satisfy the self-incurred needs. In Num.
10:33a and 11:1-3, the Jahwist has expressed his
interpretation of the Wilderness. While Jahweh's
signs and wonders continue along Israel's path
through the wilderness, the apostasy of the people
receives its just punishment.[60]

In striking contrast to the three pre-Sinaitic murmuring episodes
which result in no punishments but rather in divine assistance, the
divine wrath and punishment here are swift and sure. The different
responses, and this also holds true for the J account in Exod. 32-33,
are attributable to the seminal place of the covenant in the historiography and theology.[61] Having entered the covenant with God, on
the basis of his great saving acts, the nation is now subject to its rewards and punishments. It is this factor which reveals the systematic and consistent character of J's theology, even though there may

[60] Fritz, *Israel,* pp. 69-70.

[61] In addition to Fritz, Jay Wilcoxen ("Some Anthropocentric Aspects of Israel's
Sacred History," *Journal of Religion* 48 (1968), pp. 333-350) has also noted the importance of the Sinaitic covenant in the wilderness historiographies; but in addition
to failing to distinguish the successive sources, he draws conclusions from the structure which are so speculative that they can neither be affirmed nor denied; G. Coats,
"The Wilderness Itinerary," *CBQ* 34 (1972), p. 150n, in response to Wilcoxen, admits the seminal place of Sinai, but he does not relate this to the retributive theology.

be subordinate patterns.[62] The fact that this pattern in J has been unobserved for so long may be attributed not only to the displacements of his account by later sources, but also to the nature of his art, which, while it is paradigmatic, is not as explicitly paradigmatic as the later sources. J does not stop to explain and exhort but allows the portrayal to speak for itself. We shall say more of this in our consideration of J as a theologian. The last episode seems to indicate a collective retribution; although it implies that all of "the people" complained, only some of them are punished.[63]

The next murmuring episode occurs immediately:

> Now the rabble that was among them had a strong craving; and the people of Israel wept again, and said: "O that we had meat to eat! We remember the fish we ate in Egypt for nothing, the cucumbers, the melons, the beets, the onions, and the garlic; but now our strength is dried up, and there is nothing at all but this manna to look at."[64]

Now the miraculous manna is rejected, and the nation looks back longingly to Egypt, forgetting its cruel servitude from which it has been delivered in response to its own prayer. The ingratitude of

---

[62] For example, the distinction between the character of the pre-Sinaitic incidents and that of the post-Sinaitic, noted by Fritz (*Israel,* p. 35), is also mentioned by Childs (*Exodus,* pp. 258-260) but the latter fails to take note of the covenant, inferring instead that the episodes rewarded reflect "natural needs" while those punished issue from "imaginary needs."

[63] Freedman, in "Divine Commitment and Human Obligation: The Covenant Theme" (*Interpretation* 18, 1964), pp. 427-428, rightly notes that "while the commandments are addressed to the individual and require individual compliance, it is the community which is answerable to God for the actions of its members; only in rare instances does God deal directly with covenant violators; the community is the legally constituted agency of his judgment"; also: H. Wheeler Robinson, *Corporate Personality in Ancient Israel* (rev. ed.; Philadelphia: Fortress, 1980), p. 51; and compare: George E. Mendenhall, *The Tenth Generation: The Origins of the Biblical Tradition* (Baltimore: Johns Hopkins, 1973), pp. 113-114.

[64] Num. 11:4-6; analyses of chapter 11 vary slightly but there is a basic consensus according to Fritz (*Israel,* pp. 16-70), the following sections are J: vv. 4-6, 10, 13, 18-24a, 31-35; according to Coats (*Rebellion,* pp. 96-98) the following are probably J: vv. 1-6, 10-15, 18-23, 31-34; according to Noth (*Numbers,* p. 83) the following are probably J: 4-13, 18-24a, 31-34; and see: H. Seebass, "Num. XI, XII und die Hypothese des Jahwisten," *VT* 28 (1978), pp. 214-223.

Noth offers the cogent explanation that since the account of murmuring in Exod. 16 did replace the J account, this J account in Num. 11 is "an impressive intensification of the people's murmurings" and that "quails is probably an intentional advance on the manna story as an indication of God's anger." Cf. his *Numbers,* pp. 85-91; and Coats, *Rebellion,* pp. 99-100.

the people is emphasized as well as their shortsightedness with the result that the "anger of the Lord blazed."[65] He says to Moses:

> You have wept in the hearing of the Lord, saying "Who will give us meat to eat? For it was well with us in Egypt." Therefore the Lord will give you meat, and you shall eat. You shall not eat one day, or two days, or five days, or ten days, or twenty days, but a whole month, until it comes out at your nostrils, and becomes loathsome to you, because you have rejected the Lord who is among you, and have wept before him, saying, "Why did we come forth out of Egypt?"[66]

The craving is indulged but the indulgence itself, due to its magnitude, is a punishment.[67] Moreover, the people are punished twice: "While the meat was yet between their teeth, before it was consumed, the anger of the Lord was kindled against the people, and the Lord smote the people with a very great plague."[68] Here again the principle of collective liability seems to be determinate, but this remains problematic, since there is no indication as to who is punished although "the rabble" among them is alleged to have murmured.

The original elements of Chapter 12 are either J or an early supplement to J.[69] Miriam and Aaron speak against Moses because of his Cushite wife.[70] The Lord is angered and Miriam is punished with leprosy, but it is then cured by God at Moses' intercession.[71]

The spy episode recounted in Num. 13:14 is of great importance

---

[65] Num. 11:10.

[66] *Ibid.,* 11:18-20.

[67] Coats, *Rebellion,* pp. 114-115.

[68] Num. 11:33; although Coats (*Rebellion,* pp. 114-115) regards this as secondary, Noth (*Numbers,* p. 81) and Fritz (*Israel,* pp. 74-75) agree that this is part of the J account.

[69] According to Fritz (*Israel,* p. 19), the original J content is vv. 1, 9a, 10ab, 13-16; in the view of Noth (*Pentateuchal Traditions,* pp. 126-127) the original narrative, Miriam's rebellion, the Lord's anger and her punishment, are probably J, while the challenge to Moses' prophetic office is an addition; elsewhere Noth (*Numbers,* p. 94) expresses the view that the chapter as it stands may be an early supplement to J but that the original J content cannot be ascertained because of the conflation; he infers that the supplement is early because it represents a state in which Aaron is still not recognized as Moses' brother and helper.

[70] Num. 12:1a.

[71] Num. 12:9a, 10ab, 13-16.

from the perspective of the later sources. It is here that the land theme is brought explicitly within the covenant theology of J and the conditionality of its possession within that framework is secured.[72] Moses orders the land reconnoitered to ascertain its value and the nature and strength of the Canaanite inhabitants. The spies report that the land is bounteous, but that its dwellers are strong and their cities fortified. They are afraid and do not wish to fight against them. "And the people wept that night" and "they said to one another, 'Let us choose a captain and go back to Egypt.' "[73] The Lord is angered, and says to Moses: "How long will this people despise me?" and in response swears that with regard to the land, "none of those who despise me shall see it."[74] By virtue of the last half verse, ascribed by all to J, the land is explicitly brought within the retributive system of J which derives from the covenant. The Promise to the Patriarchs is now rendered conditional, and from this small but highly significant beginning, the land gradually becomes, in the subsequent historiographies, *the* fundamental element in the evolving theology. We may note in anticipation that in the J account only those who despise the Lord will be excluded, but the consequences of this are not clear in their details.

When Moses reports this to the people "they mourned greatly," but by the next morning they disregard the Lord's sentence, saying, "See, we are here, we will go up to the place which the Lord has promised, for we have sinned;"[75] *i.e.,* they have sinned in doubting and wanting to return to Egypt. But now Moses warns against the assault; the dangers seen by the spies will not be overcome since the Lord is no longer with them. Moreover, to attempt an assault now would constitute a further transgression. But the people go anyway, leaving Moses, only to face the Amalekites and the Canaanites, who "came down, and defeated them, and pursued them even to Hormah."[76] In this episode also, the nature of the retributive

---

[72] There is fundamental agreement as to which elements are to be ascribed to the J account: Noth (*Numbers,* pp. 101-102), 13:17b-20, 22-24, 27-31, 14:4, 11ff; Fritz (*Israel,* p. 23), 13, 17b-20, 22-24, 26bb, 27-31, 14:1b, 4, 8, 9, 11-25, 39-45; Coats (*Rebellion,* p. 139), 13: 17b-20, 22a (22b), 23-24, 27-28 (29), 30-31, 14-1b, 4, 11a (11b-23a), 23b-24 (25a), 25b, 39-45.

[73] Num. 14:1b,4.

[74] *Ibid.,* 14:11-a, 23b.

[75] *Ibid.,* 14:40.

[76] *Ibid.,* 14:44-45.

system of J is problematic. It is "the people," which seems to imply the entire contingent, who transgressed, but whether those who "despised" the Lord means all the people is not clear.

At this point begins the wilderness wandering period, the duration of which remains as yet unspecified. This theme is taken up below.

The story of Dathan and Abiram in Num. 16 is ascribed to J, with the Korah story, which does not alter the structure, subsequently woven into it.[77] The two men accuse Moses of murder, of taking them "out of the land flowing with milk and honey" to kill them in the Wilderness, and of ambition, of deceiving them to make himself "a prince over us."[78] Angry, Moses states that he has not led them of his own volition, but rather because "the Lord has sent me to do all these works."[79] He predicts that he will be vindicated by the unique way in which the rebels will be punished: "They will go down alive to Sheol and then you shall know that these men have despised the Lord." Moses' prediction proves correct.[80]

The refusal of the King of Edom to grant Israel passage through his land in Num. 20:14-21 is not of importance for this study, but is noteworthy because it is the first instance in the book where E is clearly in evidence.[81]

At Hormah the people are opposed by the king of Akad who captures some of them. Enslaved, they make a vow that if the Lord helps them defeat their enemies, they will put their cities to the ban. God grants them the victory, and the people keep their vow.[82] The source of this episode is obscure, possibly originally J or an originally independent story.[83] Its problematic origin notwithstanding, the episode does figure prominently in subsequent historiographies so it is noted here. There is no murmuring, but there is reward for faithfulness.

---

[77] Noth, *Numbers,* pp. 120, 121, 123; Coats, *Rebellion,* pp. 156, 160; Fritz, *Israel,* p. 25.

[78] Num. 16:12-14.

[79] *Ibid.,* 16-28.

[80] *Ibid.,* 16:31-34.

[81] Noth, *Numbers,* p. 149.

[82] Num. 21:1-3.

[83] Noth, *Numbers,* p. 154; Fritz, *Israel,* p. 29.

The story of the serpents in Num. 21 is similarly problematic in origin.[84] It does, however, report a rebellion and punishment. The people "became impatient" when they left Edom,[85] which constitutes an act of faithlessness. In v. 4, which may be E,[86] they again accuse Moses of bringing them out of Egypt to die in the Wilderness. In response, the Lord punishes them by sending fiery serpents "so that many of the people of Israel died."[87] The people repent, Moses prays for their pardon and the remaining people are forgiven.[88]

In an episode which may be E but which certainly contains E elements, Israel utterly defeats Shihon, the king of the Amorites.[89] This episode contains no murmuring.

The episode of apostasy in Num. 25 might be ascribed to J but it is "scarcely self-contained" and the chapter itself is "remarkably inconsequential and fragmentary."[90] At Shittim the daughters of Moab invite the people to sacrifice to their gods, among them Baal of Peor. The Lord is angered and orders Moses to hang all of the chiefs to avert his wrath. Moses orders the judges to slay all the idolatrous.[91] This is the last of the episodes of disobedience in the Book of Numbers.

In conclusion, there is ample reason to infer that J's wilderness historiography does contain a consistent retributive theology. All the episodes that can clearly be attributed to J reflect this system. These episodes which may be conflated by early additions to the J narrative, i.e., early supplements to J, and E, also conform to J's retributive system. In light of J's demonstrable consistency, and the consistency of the conflated episodes, a consistent and comprehensive retributive theology seems clearly to exist in J, while it certainly exists in J and E taken together. Moreover, this retributive theology is based on the Sinaitic covenant; before it, no incidents of mur-

[84] Fritz (*Israel,* p. 30) regards it as J; Coats (*Rebellion,* p. 117) regards it as "a late secondary insertion into the pentateuchal complex"; Noth (*Pentateuchal Traditions,* p. 121) states that it "probably constitutes an addition to the work of J."

[85] Num. 21:4.

[86] Coats, *Rebellion,* p. 117; Noth, *Numbers,* pp. 155-158.

[87] Num. 21:6.

[88] *Ibid.,* 21:7-9.

[89] Fritz, *Israel,* p. 33; Noth, *Numbers,* p. 162.

[90] Noth, *Numbers,* p. 195; cf. also Coats, "The Wilderness Itinerary," p. 149n.

[91] Num. 25:1-5.

muring or disobedience are punished; after it, all are punished. In anticipation, the subsequent historiographies, without exception, conform to this pattern. With the Sinaitic covenant, the unconditional Promise to the Patriarchs of the land[92] is rendered conditional.[93] The fulfillment of the promise now depends on the obedience of the nation and its adherence to the Sinaitic covenant. Those who enter the land are the remnant of the contingent which left Egypt, minus those who have been lethally chastised for disobedience in the Wilderness. This is not to say that this remnant represents the faithful, those who did not participate in the various murmurings. Because of the lack of precision in the murmuring episodes, it is not possible to correlate exactly those who rebelled with those who were punished. But it does seem reasonable to assume that there is no exact correlation. The absence of it is attributable to the collective character of J's system of retribution. Due to this collective or national responsibility, the punishment of some represents the punishment of all. Then too, there are examples of atonement which terminate punishments in progress. Thus the contingent which enters the land is not innocent but appears as sinful as those who were caused to perish along the way for iniquity. In any event, there is no reason to assume that a generation other than that which left Egypt enters the land. This is the view, which should be noted in anticipation, of the Deuteronomic wilderness historiography of the late seventh century.

Related to the foregoing is the duration of the wilderness period. This seems to be of unspecified duration and the duration appears to have little theological significance. Noth is of the opinion that the 40-year duration of the Wilderness period was part of the tradition from its inception; and a similar view is held by McEvenue.[94]

---

[92] Claus Westermann, *The Promise to the Fathers* (Philadelphia: Fortress, 1980), pp. 28-29, 130-131.

[93] Thus unacceptable is the view of H. Wolff, in "Kerygma of J" (*Vitality of Old Testament Traditions,* p. 61), that the brief treatment of the covenant at Sinai is attributable to the fact that "by a covenant, Yahweh validates for the whole of Israel everything that was valid for the Patriarchs."

[94] Martin Noth, *Überlieferungsgeschichtliche Studien* (3rd ed.; Tübingen: Niemeyer, 1967), p. 21; S. McEvenue states that "the 40 years of blessing in the desert is not an invention of Dtr. but rather a time-honored tradition. Exodus 16:35 (JE) has Israel eating manna in the desert for 40 years, and Amos 2:10 has Yahweh lead Israel in the desert for 40 years, in order to give them the land of the Amorites; "A Source-Critical Problem in Numbers 14:26-38," *Biblica* 43 (1962), p. 455; but Exod. 16:35 is P and the mentions of 40 years in Amos are probably Deuteronomic additions.

But the "Short Historical Credo" in Deut. 26, does not mention the Wilderness and thus indicates no duration at all and the recitation of the great saving acts in Josh. 24 states only that "you lived in the wilderness a long time."[95] Both passages are held to be cultic and of great antiquity and thus if an exact duration had been established, its omission from the cultic recitation of the great saving acts would indeed be anomalous. Neither the forty year duration nor any other exact duration for the wilderness period is given by J or E.

Before considering J as a theologian, it is necessary to say a word or two about the process of formation of the historical tradition found in J. Noth fixes the formative stages of the Pentateuchal traditions during the era of the tribal confederacy, after the occupation of the arable land in Palestine but before the formation of the state.[96] An "all-Israelite" perspective is presupposed by the formation of the narrative tradition, a perspective which reflects the experience of the time of composition.

But this perspective is the creation of that later period and this "common Israelite consciousness cannot be derived simply from a common history experienced by the twelve tribes before their occupation of the land, for such a history never existed."[97] During this process of political unification, the real or imagined cultically commemorated experiences of the individual tribes or clans were gradually incorporated into a linear sequence embodying the new "all-Israelite" perspective.[98] The entelechy of this process is, as for later sources, the interaction of the principle that that which is, always was, which we shall call the principle of consistency, and conversely, the interpretation of that which is in terms of that which was. This interaction expresses itself in the sequence of successive historical-theological configurations. And this is as true for the early formation of the Pentateuchal traditions as it is for Dtr.

The fundamental motifs around which the tradition was elaborated were the "deliverance from Egypt" and "guidance into the arable land".[99] Both of these were commemorated in the cults and

---

[95] Deut. 26:5b-9; Josh. 24:2b-13.

[96] Noth, *Pentateuchal Traditions, passim.*

[97] *Ibid.,* p. 259.

[98] *Ibid.,* pp. 254-259.

[99] *Ibid.,* p. 47.

continued to be, long after their inclusion in the evolving unified narrative tradition.[100] The emerging linear sequence retained the cultic-commemorative character and their preservation is attested to by the modifications effected in the interpretation of these events during the process of incorporation. What remains axiomatic is the fact that rituals are more tenacious than myths. The latter tend to modify in accord with the dictates of the evolving present. In this case, for example, the land motif, in Noth's view, "the most comprehensive Pentateuchal theme," was connected with the cycles of the Canaanite agricultural year, but it was given a new significance to comport with the new circumstances; before this the festivals had been purely agrarian.[101] The same is true for the Passover, originally a shepherd ritual connected with the annual change of pastures.[102] These cults were no doubt commemorations of seasonal, cyclical events or possessed this character to at least some degree.

With the amalgamation of the tribes, an elementary linear cultic recitation sequence evolved in the form of a "Short Historical Credo."[103] The wilderness motif is a secondary addition to the two original motifs, added for aetiological reasons, to fill the historical gap between the two primary events of *Heilgeschichte.*[104] At the same time, "it was necessary to bridge the geographical gap between the southern Wilderness and the land of East Jordan.[105] Into this motif all manner of individual tales of terror in the Wilderness were incorporated, tales which not only comported with but enhanced its original theological prestige, magnifying the great saving acts of Jahweh in the midst of a series of natural obstacles, lack of food, water, *etc.*[106]

The murmuring motif, as it now appears, is commonly regarded as an addition to the wilderness motif, but that is the limit of scholarly consensus. Noth judges it the result of the extension from one incident to all others, its consistency indicating a pre-literary inclu-

[100] *Ibid.,* pp. 190, 196, 197.

[101] von Rad, *Old Testament Theology,* II, p. 104.

[102] Noth, *Pentateuchal Traditions,* pp. 67-68.

[103] von Rad, *Problem of the Hextateuch,* pp. 2, 104.

[104] Noth, *Pentateuchal Traditions,* p. 206.

[105] *Ibid.*

[106] *Ibid.,* pp. 190-193; Coats, *Rebellion,* pp. 152, 155.

sion in the narrative.[107] At the other end of the spectrum is Fritz
who regards it as, by and large, the creation of J, as a warning to
the new monarchy in the form of a didactic history.[108] Schmid views
it as the creation of J, but regards J as more a process than a person
and places its culmination in the late seventh century, attributing it
to Deuteronomic circles.[109] Coats ascribes its extension to J but is
constrained by his interpretation of it as a polemic of Judah against
Israel, to accord it a very late date.[110] De Vries considers it the result
of a "theological reflex" effected to coordinate conquest traditions.[111] The fact that what J inherited and what J contributed cannot be resolved with certainty constitutes a formidable impediment
to any evaluation of J as an historian and theologian. Taking J's
account as it appears, however, and looking specifically at the theological and philosophical evaluation of man contained in the wilderness archetype, despite its consistent causal connections between
obedience and reward, disobedience and punishment, the student
does not find polemics, preachments or paradigms of idyllic times.
This is partly attributable to J's penchant for portrayal instead of
explanation and discussion, and also to the fact that his portrayal
depicts man's condition as irremediable.[112] J's account is one of the
most dismal portrayals of man in world literature. The grandeur of
his portrayal is pervaded by a profound somberness as man's insatiability, mendacity and ingratitude are displayed with a relentless
irony which follows his itinerary from one folly to the next.[113] The
exhortation of principles and practices is virtually precluded by the

[107] Noth, *Pentateuchal Traditions,* pp. 124-125; Coats also stresses this unity of
the motif ("The Wilderness Itinerary," in *CBQ* 34, 1972, p. 149n): "The murmuring tradition holds together as a single negative interpretation of the wilderness period."

[108] Fritz, *Israel,* pp. 112-122.

[109] Schmid, *Der Sogenannte Jahwist* (Zürich: Theologischer Verlag, 1976), pp.
77-79, 117, 130, 157, 166-167.

[110] Coats, *Rebellion,* pp. 250-251.

[111] S. J. de Vries, "The Origins of the Murmuring Tradition," *JBL* 87 (1968), p.
58.

[112] Speiser (*Genesis,* pp. XXI. XXVII), whose view we share that "we have in J
. . . not only the most gifted biblical writer, but one of the greatest figures in world
literature," notes also that "while E has a tendency to justify and explain events, J
allows people's actions to speak for themselves."

[113] Cf. M. L. Henry, *Jahwist und Priesterschaft: Zwei Glaubenszeugnisse; Arbeiten zur Theologie* Heft 3 (Stuttgart: Calwer, 1960).

ferocious irony of the portrayal. A most profound pessimism in the face of the irremediable sinfulness of man is evident through his narrative. The wilderness portrayal becomes increasingly sardonic as the murmurings continue in the lengthening wake of blessings and punishments. The apparent victim of his own insatiability, man courts his own destruction but remains oblivious to it. There is no Deuteronomic or prophetic fervor here.

In J's ironic detachment, however, the ferocity of disillusionment can still be discerned. This underlies the narrative's relentlessly logical and theological consistency. There is in J but a slight concern with ethical matters of a more prosaic order such as theft, adultery and the oppression of widows and orphans. J's concerns are more basic, implicitly recognizing the innate spirituality of man and yet concerned with the sources of his own moral sensibilities, a concern evidenced by his inclusion, in his primeval history, of an explanation for the existence of moral consciousness itself. J is a pious man who has reflected on his own moral sensibilities and tends toward fatalism in his inability to render an unambiguous answer.

One might, of course, contend that J inherited this view of man from the extant narrative traditions of the Wilderness, which he simply recorded, and then added the primeval history in the same spirit. This is doubtful, for although J may have inherited some part of the murmuring motif, a theology as unremittingly somber and pessimistic as his would be anomalous in popular narrative since it would tend not to thrive on such gloomy portrayals. Such a grim outlook as this more likely issues from an unusual individual temperament, whose observations of men and events are not mechanically derived from previous sources. We are inclined to share the view of Speiser that a "work with such distinctive personal traits could stem only from an individual author."[114] For the foregoing reasons, together with the arguments of Fritz, we regard the murmuring motif as principally the contribution of J.[115]

Adhering to the commonly accepted mid-10th century date for J, we also share Fritz's interpretation of the Wilderness as a warning to the new monarchy in the form of a didactic history.[116] Yet, J's

[114] Speiser, *Genesis,* p. XXVIII.

[115] Fritz, *Israel,* pp. 117-122.

[116] *Ibid.,* p. 122; but cf. Schulte (*Die Entstehung der Geschichtsschreibung im Alten Testament*) who dates it somewhat later and interprets it somewhat differently,

portrayal of man is so relentlessly pessimistic that it leaves little hope for man in any period. But there is no conclusive evidence for J in this period. The arguments of those who have placed J very much later are considered below.

While the foregoing considerations are somewhat problematic, the retributive theology of J's wilderness historiography is quite clear. It is important to mention that the land is for J the reward to the nation as a collective entity, and of course it is a material reward, symbolizing peace and material prosperity.

although regarding it as didactic history; and Werner Schmidt, "Ein Theologe in Salomonischer Zeit? Plädoyer für den Jahwisten," *BZ* 25 (1981), pp. 96-102.

4: The Elohist Wilderness Historiography

J wrote his history during the period of the monarchy, perhaps at its zenith, and recounted in it the continuous history of humanity, including his explanation for the acquisition of the land which was not only still possessed, but had reached the limits of its expansion. E is customarily dated about a century later, although it had formerly been dated in the eighth century. Originally an independent source, its preservation is so fragmentary that far less can be said of its character than can be said of J which was used as the main source when J and E were joined by a redactor, probably in the seventh century. E is usually held to be of northern origin.[117]

The preservation of E is especially fragmentary in the wilderness historiography except for its covenant which appears to be more extensive and detailed than the J covenant which it displaces. The character of the displacement, and the scattered and very fragmentary instances of E in the wilderness (aside from Sinai, which E calls Horeb), and the instances where E has been closely interwoven with J, support the inference that E comports with the retributive struc-

---

[117] Ruppert, "Der Elohist - Sprecher für Gottes Volk," *Wort und Botschaft,* p. 110; Wolff, "The Elohist Fragments in the Pentateuch," *The Vitality of Old Testament Traditions,* p. 81; T. E. Fretheim, "Elohist," *IDB Supp.,* pp. 259-263.

ture of the J wilderness historiography. The clearest example of E, aside from its covenant, is the Golden Calf episode in Exod. 32-33, which is commonly interpreted as a polemic against the cult established by Jeroboam in Israel soon after the division of the empire of Solomon into two kingdoms. This interpretation is acceptable although, as shown, a J episode of sin and punishment underlies the superimposition of the E account. Various efforts have been made to find differences in the characters of the J and E theologies,[118] but the retributive structures expressed in their wilderness historiographies appear identical. While it is true that the land does not figure prominently in E, the conditionality of its possession may be inferred from the Golden Calf episode and its punishment, and from those instances in which J and E have inextricably intertwined.

Whether written during the reign of Jeroboam or in the century following it, E can be interpreted as a polemic against idolatrous practice common throughout the period.[119] But whether resurgent Assyria was regarded as the judgment of God[120] is questionable and to a large degree dependent on E's date. In the ninth century the Assyrian threat was rather remote; in the eighth century it had become eminently real.

J and E taken together, as joined by the JE redactor, exhibit a retributive theology in their wilderness historiography which is striking in its consistency. The source of this consistency is the J account of the Wilderness, which comprises the most extensive material in the JE account.

---

[118] Most recently A. W. Jenks, *The Elohist and North Israelite Traditions, JBL Mon. Ser.* 22 (Missoula: Scholars Press, 1977), esp. pp. 66-67.

[119] Wolff, "The Elohist," p. 81.

[120] Ruppert, "Elohist," p. 117.

5: The Wilderness in Pre-Exilic Prophecy

The estimate of the wilderness generation in the eighth century book of the prophet Amos differs markedly from those of J and E. Amos mentions the deliverance from Egypt as evidence of the omnipotence and favor of the Lord: "O people of Israel, amongst the whole family which I brought up out of the land of Egypt: 'You only I have known of all the families of the earth; therefore I will punish you for all your iniquities.' "[121] Not only did the Lord deliver them, but he destroyed the Amorites and gave the nation their land as a possession.[122] In connection with the deliverance and gift of the land, the wilderness period is mentioned twice, as another example of divine power and favor. For the first time the period is given a specific duration of forty years,[123] but this is regarded as a late, probably Deuteronomic, addition.[124]

[121] Amos, 3:1-2.

[122] *Ibid.,* 2:9-11.

[123] *Ibid.,* 2:10; 5:25.

[124] James L. Mays, *Amos: A Commentary, OTL* (Philadelphia: Westminster, 1969), pp. 51, 111; Hans Walter Wolff, *Joel and Amos,* (Philadelphia: Fortress, 1977), pp. 44, 42, 112, 170, 175, also argues that the mention of the wilderness in Amos (2:10-12) is a Deuteronomic addition.

Amos does not offer an explicit estimate of the character of the wilderness generation, but it is clear from 5:25 that he held it in high regard. The prophet, piqued by the detailed and ostentatious fulfillment of the cultic law, in contravention of its spirit, asks rhetorically: "Did you bring to me sacrifices and offerings the forty years in the wilderness, O house of Israel."[125] The clear implication is that the wilderness generation fulfilled the spirit, rather than the letter of the law. The refrain, "yet you did not return to me," which follows the enumeration of blessings and punishments, also implies faithfulness during a former period. What is clear, however, is that Amos' estimate of the wilderness generation differs radically from those of J (and E).

Thus Amos appears to know nothing of the murmurings and punishments in the Wilderness. For him that period, along with the Exodus and Conquest, constitutes an archetype of divine favor.[126] He employs another incident as an archetype of punishment, that of Sodom and Gomorrah.[127] Thus there are several common elements in Amos and in JE: Sodom and Gomorrah, the election tradition, the Exodus, the Wilderness and the Conquest. On the basis of these common elements, Davies concludes that an awareness of JE by Amos may be inferred.[128] While the other elements would have been common knowledge, and common to both the JE literary tradition and the popular narrative tradition, the JE wilderness historiography is the one element found only in that JE source. Amos' apparent unfamiliarity with that single element is clear evidence of his independence from the JE literary tradition, showing that he relied instead on other sources, popular, cultic, or both.

Moreover, there is no evidence of a covenant relation in Amos by which the nation is obligated to obey. Instead, and we concur with the argument of Perlitt, the obligation appears to arise from the great saving acts themselves.[129]

---

[125] Amos, 5:25.

[126] Cf. Ch. Barth, "Zur Bedeutung der Wüstentradition," p. 19.

[127] Amos, 4:10-11.

[128] G. H. Davies, "The Yahwistic Tradition in the Eighth Century Prophets," in H. H. Rowley, ed., *Studies in Old Testament Prophecy Presented to Professor Theodore H. Robinson* (Edinburgh: Clark, 1950), pp. 44-45.

[129] Perlitt, *Bundestheologie,* pp. 136-150; North, *Old Testament Interpretation of History,* p. 53; R. E. Clements, *Prophecy and Covenant, SBT* 43 (Naperville: Allenson, 1965), pp. 45-85, esp. 55; Nicholson, *Exodus and Sinai,* pp. 76-77, 82; Clements, *Prophecy and Tradition* (Atlanta: John Knox, 1975), pp. 17-21.

The estimate of the wilderness generation of the late eighth century prophet Hosea is similar to that of Amos: "I am the Lord your God, from the land of Egypt."[130] In Hosea the wilderness period is given no specific duration and does not figure at all, as in Amos, as one of the great saving acts which form the basis of the obligation to obey. But the deliverance from Egypt is alluded to repeatedly, and a positive estimate of the Wilderness is in evidence: The Lord threatens to return the nation to the Wilderness "and there she shall answer as in the days of her youth, as at the time when she came out of the land of Egypt."[131] But in contrast to Amos the innocence of the nation does not endure throughout the period: "Like grapes in the wilderness, I found Israel. Like the first fruit on the fig tree, in its first season, I saw your fathers. But they came to Ba'al-pe'or, and consecrated themselves to Ba'al, and became detestable like the thing they loved."[132] Here the former innocence appears to terminate in the Wilderness, but the Ba'al-pe'or incident which occurs in Num. 25 is the last instance of rebellion in the Wilderness and, as noted, it may be a supplement to J. Moreover, as Andersen and Freedman note, 'Baal-Peor does not belong to the Wilderness period, but marks the beginning of Israel's decline through contact with the Canaanite cultures.''[133] Hosea's reference to it does not constitute proof of his reliance on JE since he has a positive estimate of the wilderness experience to that point and this differs markedly from JE. Moreover, Mendenhall observes that Hosea gives the Baal-Peor incident "a very interesting variant which has no basis in our narrative and can only come from ancient traditions of another source."[134] The reference in chapter 11 is highly problematic: "When Israel was a child I loved him and out of Egypt I called my son. But the more I called them, the more they went from me; they kept sacrificing to the Ba'als, and burning incense to idols."[135] This may refer either to the Ba'al-pe'or incident

[130] Hos. 12:9.

[131] Hos. 2:14-15.

[132] *Ibid.,* 9:10.

[133] Francis I. Andersen and David Noel Freedman, *Hosea* (AB; NY: Doubleday, 1980), p. 166.

[134] Mendenhall, *Tenth Generation,* p. 106; Andersen and Freedman, *Hosea,* pp. 75, 630; Schmidt, "Ein Theologe in Salomonischer Zeit?", p. 98.

[135] Hos. 11:1-2.

or to a later degeneration ensuing after the occupation of the land.

The existence of a covenant in Hosea (1:9, 6:7, 8:1) has been affirmed and denied, but the evidence for it is strong; explicit reliance of Hosea on the covenant seems clear, though somewhat problematic.[136]

Jenks has argued convincingly that instead of direct literary dependence of Hosea on E, the prophet "made free and frequent use of the common epic traditions which were still vital and far richer than we would expect on the basis of our written Pentateuch alone."[137] The same author regards Hosea's negative references to the Wilderness as a radical reinterpretation of the Exodus based on the "ancient tradition of Israel's murmuring and rebellion there."[138] This is not, however, a reinterpretation; rather, it is similar, but only in small part, to the JE portrayal upon which Hosea does not seem to have a direct dependence.[139] Moreover, Jenks's view that Hosea's estimate of the Wilderness is "peculiarly prophetic and northern" cannot be sustained when compared with J's wilderness historiography. But for this period, Jenks's interpretation is true enough. Hosea's explicit references to the covenant are somewhat anomalous in pre-exilic prophecy and this remains to be explained.

In Isaiah there is no explicit or implicit mention of the Wilderness. The theme of degeneration is present but this degeneration seems to date from some time after the occupation of the land: "Sons, I have reared and brought up, but they have rebelled against me, they have foresaken the Lord."[140] This implies a period of faithfulness, the period of the monarchy, or perhaps the time of David only[141] or an earlier period under "your judges as at the first, and your counsellors as at the beginning."[142] There is no clear refer-

---

[136] Perlitt, *Bundestheologie,* pp. 146-150; and Jenk's view of "Hosea's strong emphasis on the Covenant," *Elohist,* p. 114; Walther Eichrodt, *Theology of the Old Testament* (Philadelphia: Westminster, 1967), I, p. 51; Hans Walter Wolff, *Hosea: A Commentary* (Philadelphia: Fortress, 1974), XXIV; James Luther Mays, *Hosea, OTL* (Philadelphia: Westminster, 1969), pp. 7-10; Andersen and Freedman, *Hosea,* p. 47.

[137] Jenks, *Elohist,* p. 117.

[138] *Ibid.,* pp. 115, 116.

[139] *Ibid.*

[140] Is. 1:2,4.

[141] *Ibid.,* 1:21.

[142] *Ibid.,* 1:26.

ence either to the Wilderness or to Egypt. But there is an explicit reference to Sodom and Gomorrah which is employed as an archetype of annihilation: "If the Lord of hosts had not left us a few survivors, we should have been like Sodom, and become like Gomorrah."[143] Although Israel had fallen to Assyria, Judah continued to exist but was forced to pay tribute.

The Wilderness is not mentioned explicitly by the prophet Micah, the contemporary of Isaiah, but the basis of the obligation of the nation to the Lord here too, is the great saving acts:

> For I brought you out from the land of Egypt,
> and redeemed you from the house of bondage;
> and I sent before you Moses, Aaron and Miriam.
> O my people, remember what Balak king of Moab
> devised, and what Balaam the son of Be'z an-
> swered him, and what happened from Shittim to
> Gilgal, that you may know the saving acts of the
> Lord."[144]

The fact that no mention is made either of Aaron's role in the Golden Calf apostasy, or of his and Miriam's rebellion against Moses would seem to indicate an independence from the JE tradition and a reliance instead on a later phase of the popular narrative tradition from whose earlier phase J and E drew some of their materials. There is also the possibility that Aaron and Miriam may have been viewed negatively in the earlier oral tradition, but in Micah they are clearly employed as evidence of divine favor and concern during the wilderness period.

Jeremiah's view of the Wilderness as a period of idyllic faithfulness is similar to the estimates of the prophets already discussed.[145] Israel was devoted then, and only later did it forget the deliverance from Egypt "and went after worthlessness and became worthless."[146] "I brought you into a plentiful land, to enjoy its fruits and its good things. But when you came in you defiled my land, and made my heritage an abomination."[147]

The embellishment of the Wilderness and its magnification as

---

[143] *Ibid.,* 1:9.

[144] Mic. 6:3-5.

[145] Jer. 2:1-3a.

[146] *Ibid.,* 2:4.

[147] *Ibid.,* 2:7.

one of the miraculous saving acts do not take the form, as in Amos, of a specific and lengthy duration. Instead, the wondrousness of the divine guidance through it increased by the dramatization of the perils. In Jeremiah it is not merely the wilderness, but a "land of deserts and pits", a "land of drought and deep darkness", a "land that none passes through, where no man dwells."[148] While the dramatization is clear, its source is not. This may be the prophet's own dramatization or it may represent a later embellishment of the oral tradition. Its aim, however, is quite clear. The dangers are so magnified as to be insuperable without divine guidance. Although the Exodus is very much in evidence, Jeremiah does not allude to Sinai or to the covenant.[149]

Jeremiah employs the example of Sodom and Gomorrah three times as an archetype of absolute wickedness and consequent annihilation.[150] But as in the other pre-exilic prophets, this reference is no proof of reliance on JE; it would have been common knowledge.[151]

In summary, pre-exilic prophecy, with the very partial exception of Hosea, differs radically in its wilderness historiography from JE; it regards that period as one of perfect faithfulness. With the exception of Hosea, it does not base its exhortations to obedience explicitly on the Sinaitic covenant; but rather it seems to base the nation's obligations to Yahweh on the great saving acts of the Exodus and Wilderness traditions, acts which it magnifies.[152] The

[148] *Ibid.,* 2:6.

[149] Thus, questionable is the view of von Rad that "Jeremiah stands and acts upon the Exodus-Sinai tradition" (*Old Testament Theology,* II, p. 217); his view is shared by Bright, *Covenant and Promise,* p. 165, and by De Vaux, *Early History of Israel,* p. 418.

[150] Jer. 23:14; 49:18; 50:39.

[151] Eissfeldt, *The Old Testament,* p. 39; he notes: "The story of Sodom and Gomorrah . . . is designed to explain the unfruitfulness and desolation of the area on the banks of the southern part of the Dead Sea . . . and . . . it is also designed to explain two other curiosities, namely the existence of an apparently well-known city named Zoar presumably to be found on the southeastern shore of the Dead Sea in an area otherwise quite uninhabited."

[152] This conclusion regarding the covenant is in accord with: Perlitt, *Bundestheologie,* pp. 146-150; McCarthy, *Old Testament Covenant,* pp. 40, 78. Walter Zimmerli, "Prophetic Proclamation and Reinterpretation," in Knight, *Tradition and Theology in the Old Testament,* pp. 77-78; for a review of opinions and also modifications of his own earlier views see: R. E. Clements, *Prophecy and Tradition,* pp. 17-21; other scholars, however, have argued for obligation based on covenant in pre-exilic prophecy, for example: W. Zimmerli, *The Law and the Prophets,*

matter requires closer examination. Walther Eichrodt has addressed this problem with insight which merits consideration:

> It remains, none the less, a surprising phenomenon that throughout the period when the *classical prophets* were drastically criticizing the popular religion of Israel, the covenant concept should recede into the background . . . Even for him (Hosea) the emphasis is not in the covenant concept, but that he makes use of other categories to describe the religious relationship. Amos, Isaiah, and Micah all present it as an accepted fact that Israel's relationship with Yahweh is based on the latter's own free decision and inconceivable grace; it is only necessary to recall such passages as Amos 3:2 where the prophet is quite definitely expressing the proud conviction of the nation as a whole when he speaks of Yahweh's favor in choosing Israel above all other nations. But this makes it only the more astonishing that in precisely such passages as these, where to us the word covenant suggests itself at once, the prophets never use it.
>
> It is, however, quite out of the question to suppose that any further progress in this problem can be made simply with the scalpel of literary criticism. We must take into consideration the whole position of the prophets *vis-à-vis* the spiritual stock in trade of their nation and when this is done, the factor of decisive significance is seen to be that those reforming spirits have set themselves to oppose every instance of dead externalism in religious thought. What confronted them was an insistence on statutes and ordinances, on settled custom and usage, on the precisely organized performance of duties toward God, and a corresponding reckoning on Yahweh's automatic performance in return. An Amos inveighs strenuously against the unwearying processions and pilgrimages to famous sanctuaries and the sumptuous Temple worship; a Hosea castigates the priests for making money out of the people's

pp. 44-45, 67, 72, 92; R. E. Clements, *Prophecy and Covenant,* pp. 54-80; W. Brueggemann, *Tradition for Crisis: A Study in Hosea* (Richmond: John Knox Press, 1968), *passim.;* John Bright, *Covenant and Promise,* pp. 42, 43, 87, 112-113; regarding Amos and Hosea: E. W. Nicholson, *Deuteronomy and Tradition* (Philadelphia: Fortress, 1967), pp. 64-65.

> sense of sin and for getting fat on their offerings;
> an Isaiah stigmatizes the eager frequenting of the
> Temple and the magnificent prayers there offered
> as the "commandment" of men. In all of them
> the stress is on the personal note in the relation-
> ship to Yahweh; it is because they find this lacking
> that they insist with all the force and passion at
> their command on the ideas of honesty, of love,
> of surrender . . . In this struggle to eradicate all
> thought of an *opus operatum* the concept of the
> covenant could not help them; for as we noticed
> earlier, the weakness inherent in it which made it a
> potential danger to religious life was precisely its
> legal character.[153]

This is certainly plausible but its cogency is undermined by the repeated prophetic emphasis on the obligations based on the great saving acts. What Andersen and Freedman say of Hosea, that he denounces "the false worship of the true God and the true worship of false gods,"[154] is also true of the other pre-exilic prophets. Each of them inveighs against the legalistic perversions of Jahwism which subvert its spirit, and also against the worship of other gods. There are numerous examples of such exhortations in Hosea, Amos, Micah and Isaiah. These apostasies are violations of the essence of the covenant's supreme law: loyalty to Jahweh. Thus while pre-exilic prophecy may not base its preaching on the obligations of the Sinaitic covenant, or on the covenant concept, it clearly regards the nation as obligated to Jahweh for his past actions on its behalf, *i.e.,* the great saving acts. Punishments, defeat and destruction, predicted for failure to fulfill obligations to Jahweh, clearly support this interpretation. The system of retribution in pre-exilic prophecy is a variant of the collective responsibility in JE: Sometimes the punishment of all is promised for the transgressions of a few but at other times the punishment of all is predicted for sins which are attributed to all.[155] From the conspicuous absence of references to the covenant and the positive estimate of the Wilderness,

---

[153] Eichrodt, *Theology of the Old Testament,* I, pp. 52ff.

[154] Andersen and Freedman, *Hosea,* p. 48.

[155] Compare for example: Amos 2:4-8; 4:1-3; 5:10-12; 6:4-6; 8:4-6; 4:7-12; 5:16-17; 7:7-9; 8:2-3; 8:7-14; 9:1-4; Hosea: 2:4-5; 2:10-13; 4:1-3; 4:6-10; 5:8-11; 6:7-11; 7:12-13; 8:13-14; 9:15-17; 10:1-8; 10:13-15; Isaiah: 1:4-9; 1:12-17; 1:21-26; 2:6-8; 3:9-11; 3:25-26; 5:5-25; 9: 17-21; 10:1-11; Jer.: 2:7-17; 3:6-10; 4:5-8; 5:1-9; 5:14-18; 5:25-29; 6:13-15; 7:8-15; 8:20; Mic.: 1:4-9; 2:1-4; 3:5-12.

the inference is warranted that the pre-exilic prophets were unacquainted with the JE account. This is not to say, however, that that account was not in existence. The reasons for not attributing the JE retributive theology to the later Deuteronomic theologians are enumerated below.

6: The Wilderness Generation in the Pre-Exilic Psalter

While several psalms, notably those which reflect Deuteronomic theology and those which are clearly exilic, present few problems, there are at least two which are highly problematic as to date and content. We are inclined to regard Ps. 105 as pre-exilic, but this is of course hypothetical.[156] The psalm does deal with the Wilderness, in somewhat greater detail than pre-exilic prophecy. Its treatment of the period of the sojourn in Egypt and the Exodus is, however, quite detailed. With regard to the Wilderness, it makes no reference to the murmuring tradition but places exclusive stress on the divine favor during that phase. The guidance, manna and water are mentioned in this connection, but briefly.[157] The absence of the murmuring in this context is conspicuous. Equally conspicuous is the omission of any reference to the Sinaitic covenant. The promises to the patriarchs are unconditional.[158]

While there are common elements in JE and Ps. 105, the diver-

[156] Mitchell Dahood, *The Psalms,* AB (NY: Doubleday, 1968), III, p. 51.

[157] Ps. 105:39-42.

[158] *Ibid.,* 8:11.

gencies loom much larger. For this reason we are in agreement with Weiser who views a direct literary dependence of the psalm on the JE literary tradition as improbable.[159] But we do not share his view that the psalm is equally independent of the sources of J and E; it may be, but this remains an open question.

Weiser's interpretation of Ps. 105 applies to Ps. 136 as well. The latter recounts the saving acts and makes no mention of murmuring in the Wilderness. It states only that God "led his people through the wilderness . . . and slew famous kings . . . Sihon, king of the Amorites . . . and Og, king of Bashan . . . and gave their land as a heritage."[160] Weiser attributes this to the dependence of the JE literary tradition and the oral cultic tradition represented by the psalm on a common source, and this seems plausible.[161]

Thus, these two psalms, with very minor variants, seem to agree in their wilderness historiography with that of pre-exilic Prophecy. No murmuring is evident and the obligation of the nation to the Lord seems to issue from the great saving acts, not from a distinct covenantal relationship.

Consequently, the argument of Nicholson that the Deuteronomic covenant theology evolved in prophetic circles from the ancient (pre-monarchial and earlier) cult, cannot be accepted. Nicholson's view fails to explain the absence of the Sinaitic covenant and positive wilderness historiography of the pre-exilic Psalter.[162] It is quite possible, however, that the cultic commemoration of the covenant in Judah was eclipsed, as has been suggested, by the Davidic covenant. Up to this point, the radical differences between the wilderness historiographies of JE on the one hand, and pre-exilic Prophecy and Psalms on the other hand, would seem to strengthen the arguments of those who contend that JE dates from much later than has been supposed. In JE the Wilderness is sinful but in pre-exilic Prophecy and Psalms it is the model of faithfulness to Jahweh. A fuller examination of this apparent anomaly is in order and some clarification is supplied by the analysis of Deuteronomic theology and its wilderness historiography.[163]

---

[159] A. Weiser. *The Psalms: A Commentary, OTL* (Philadelphia: Westminster, 1961), p. 674.

[160] Ps. 136. 16-22.

[161] Weiser, *Psalms,* p. 792; cf. Fritz, *Israel.*

[162] Nicholson, *Deuteronomy and Tradition,* pp. 119-124; also DeVaux, *Early History of Israel,* p. 417, for a variant opinion.

[163] Schmid, *Der Sogenannte Jahwist,* pp. 80-81, 154-156.

7: The Deuteronomic (DT) Wilderness Historiography

Over three decades ago, Martin Noth advanced his thesis of the Deuteronomic history, a theologically unified historical corpus extending from Deuteronomy through II Kings.[164] He concluded that the history was the work of an exilic author-editor who wrote to explain the decline and destruction of the states of Israel and Judah and who explained it, theologically, as the result of "immer wachsenden Verfalls"; the author

> ... did not write his work for entertainment in hours of leisure or for the gratification of those interested in national history, but rather as a didactic about the true meaning of the history of Israel beginning with the seizure of land until the destruction of the prevailing state of affairs; the meaning of this is disclosed to him in the recognition of the fact that in this history God acted perceptibly because He responded with admonitions and punishment to the constantly growing deterioration and finally, when these were of no avail, He answered with a total destruction.[165]

---

[164] Noth, *Überlieferungsgeschichtliche Studien.*

[165] *Ibid.,* p. 100.

Noth also concluded that the work was written in a dismal spirit and left no hope for the nation.[166] Although a few scholars have retained Noth's view that there is one exilic Deuteronomic (or Deuteronomistic) history,[167] subsequent scholarship has tended to view the work as a product of at least two distinct redactions.[168] Not all scholars concur, however, and a variant view is that of Weinfeld, who states that the "Deuteronomic composition is the creation of scribal circles which began their literary project some time prior to the reign of Josiah and were still at work after the fall of Judah."[169] This view of the compositional process is plausible as regards Dt which, despite its heterogeneity, is clear and consistent concerning the generation which enters the land, and the estimate of that generation both in the land and in the Wilderness. The behavior of that generation in the Wilderness is consistently negative; in the land, consistently positive. The apparent inconsistency is resolved in Dt by the exoneration of that generation.

The subsequent modifications of Dt, which are attributed here to an exilic Dtr recension, although not extensive, are so dramatic and significant that they can clearly be distinguished from the Dt position. No exhaustive analysis of Dt or Dtr is offered here. Before considering the modifications, there should be a brief review of the relevant facts of the political history of Israel and Judah.

J wrote his history at the zenith of the Israelite empire's power and territorial expansion. Immediately following the death of Solo-

---

[166] *Ibid.*, pp. 107-110.

[167] Cf. J. A. Soggin, *Joshua: A Commentary, OTL* (Philadelphia: Westminster, 1962), pp. 3-7.

[168] This was explicitly rejected by Noth; see *Überlieferungsgeschichtliche Studien,* p. 91n; for a review of the recent scholarship see: Sigrid Loersch, *Das Deuteronomium und seine Deutung, Stuttgarter Bibelstudien* 22 (Stuttgart: Katholisches Bibelwerk, 1967); and the relevant chapter in Anderson, *Tradition and Interpretation;* A. N. Radjawane, "Das Deuteronomistische Geschichtswerk: Ein Forschungsbericht," *Theologische Rundschau* 38 (1973-74), pp. 177; A. Jepsen, *Die Quellen des Königsbuches* (Halle: Niemeyer, 1956), pp. 76, 95; R. Smend, " Das Gesetz und die Völker," in Wolff, ed., *Probleme Biblischer Theologie, Gerhard v. Rad zum 70. Geburtstag* (München: Kaiser, 1971), pp. 494-509; W. Dietrich, *Prophetie und Geschichte: Eine Redaktionsgeschichtliche Untersuchung zum Deuteronomistischen Geschichtswerk, FRLANT* 108 (Göttingen: Vandenhoeck and Ruprecht, 1972), pp. 110-148; D. N. Freedman, "The Deuteronomic History," *IDB Supp.,* pp. 226-228; Cross, *Canaanite Myth,* pp. 274, 298; Helga Weippert, "Die Deuteronomistischen Beurteilungen der Könige von Israel und Juda und das Problem der Redaktion der Königsbücher," *Biblica* 53 (1972); Gray, *I & II Kings: A Commentary* (2nd ed.; Philadelphia: Westminster, 1974), Introduction.

[169] Weinfeld, *Deuteronomy,* p. 9.

mon in 922, the empire divided into the two states of Judah and Israel. Resurgent Assyria had already begun its expansion in the ninth century and embarked on the road of systematic conquest under Tiglath-pileser III in the third quarter of the eighth century. By 742 Israel had been laid under heavy tribute. Much of the Northern Kingdom was conquered and converted into Assyrian provinces. The remainder was ruled as a vassal state of Assyria but most of that remaining portion was conquered in 724. Two years later Samaria fell and many of its inhabitants were deported. Israel had vanished. Nothing was left of the land in the Northern Kingdom.

The Southern Kingdom became a vassal state of Assyria at about the same time. But with the disintegration of Assyria about one hundred years later, it regained its independence and recovered a part of Israel. In 609 Judah fell under the domination of Egypt and in 603 became the vassal state of Babylon. In 597 Jerusalem surrendered and many leading citizens were deported to Babylon. In 587 Jerusalem was conquered and destroyed and more survivors were deported to Babylon. This marked the end of Judah and now the entire Promised Land was gone.

During this same period of political decline and defeat, despite occasional dramatic religious reforms, the religious life of Judah and Israel was characterized by repeated and apparently ineradicable apostasies from Jahwism, both official and popular. Many of these instances of apostasy are verifiable, particularly the official episodes which reflect the policies of several of the kings. The popular apostasies are more problematic and some may be creations of Deuteronomic theology, effected to render its view more consistent. That view is contained in the Book of Deuteronomy and in the Deuteronomic History, the corpus of which extends from the beginning of the Deuteronomy to the end of II Kings.

The two parallel sequences noted above, religious apostasy and political destruction, in and of themselves, bear no causal relation to each other. Their causal relation in Deuteronomic theology is simply assumed by modern biblical scholarship, which has tended to address itself more to the geographical, chronological and institutional provenances of that theology than to its theological sources. Thus the contention of von Rad that northern Levitical circles are the sources of Deuteronomic theology has been sustained by some authorities and questioned by others, although a northern

provenance is usually accepted.[170] The failure to address the problem of the theological sources of Deuteronomic theology is partly
attributable to the common view, previously discussed, that the
earlier sources, JE, do not contain a consistent retributive theology. It has been argued in this paper that this inveterate opinion is
mistaken. Now the argument is advanced that the Deuteronomic
causal relation between sin and political defeat derives from the interpretation of these two distinct sequences in terms of the JE system of retribution expressed in JE's interpretation of similar phenomena of the earlier period. Deuteronomic theology is of course
dependent on the facts recorded by JE, some of which it reinter-
prets. But more important than this is the dependence on the interpretation of those facts in JE. David N. Freedman has rightly noted
that the "classic view, that Deuteronomy presupposes JE, remains
defensible."[171] But a stronger argument may be made: The Deuteronomic theology is the product of the extension of the JE retributive system to subsequent events. The theological structures, although differing in a few details, are identical. Moreover, interpreted in terms of the JE retributive system, the parallel sequences of
apostasy and political decline appeared to confirm the truth of that
JE theology. The increasingly catastrophic character of the political sequence imparted an exclusive and unparalled authority to JE
and engendered the atmosphere of urgency in the later theology. It
is this authority of JE, continually enhanced by lengthening sequences of sin and increasing political punishment, within the context of a nation incapable of faithfulness and apparently unwitting-
ly bent on its own destruction, that to a large degree explains the
fundamentalist fervor of the Deuteronomic school and its characteristic hortatory and rhetorical style. The reality portrayed by JE

---

[170] von Rad, *Old Testament Theology,* II, pp. 71-75; Odil Steck, "Theological
Strains of Tradition," in Knight, *Tradition and Theology in the Old Testament,* pp.
202-203; for variants of this view see: H. W. Wolff, "Hosea's geistige Heimat," *Gesammelte Studien* (München: Kaiser, 1964), pp. 232-250; E. W. Nicholson, *Deuteronomy and Tradition,* pp. 73-82; 94; for a summary of relevant views see Anderson,
Tradition and Interpretation, pp. 141-145.

[171] Freedman, "The Deuteronomic History," *IDB Supp.,* p. 226; Jenks (*Elohist,*
p. 121) has recently argued that "there is good reason to think that the Deuteronomic understanding of history, which is so similar, developed, through centuries of
use in covenant-renewal and similar ceremonies, directly out of this Elohistic understanding of history"; but the same author (p. 119) asserts that "in both the historical
and legal sections Deuteronomy is demonstrably dependent on earlier formulations
of tradition, but not exclusively dependent on either our J or our E."

was one which could not be denied, and denial was already producing disastrous consequences.

The original law book of Deuteronomy, *i. e.,* chapters 12-26 of the book as we now have it, was probably promulgated in the period of the reform of King Josiah in the late seventh century. The book itself with its diversified content is the product of a long period of evolution.[172] Added to the book at about the time of its promulgation was an introduction, chapters 5-11 and 28. These chapters are not a unity and do exhibit signs of a process of growth.[173] The evolution of 5-11 and 28 lies beyond our present concern. While there is substantial agreement among scholars regarding the above chapters, there is much less concerning chapters 1-4. These chapters, or most of their content, comprise not only the later introduction to the Book of Deuteronomy but also the introduction to the Deuteronomi(sti)c history which includes Deuteronomy and extends to the end of II Kings. There is little consensus regarding their contents and the dates of these contents. With very few exceptions, scholarly opinion lies between the original view of Martin Noth that chapters 1-3 (4) are the exilic introduction to the Deuteronomi(sti)c history which is an exilic work[174] and that of Cross who maintains that that history is largely a pre-exilic composition with exilic additions.[175]

In view of this essay's limited scope, the following hypotheses are offered regarding chapters 1-4: Those passages in Deut. 1-3 which concern the curse of the wilderness generation, 1:34-40 and 2:14-16, are exilic and differ radically in some respects, from the view of that generation in chapters 5-11 and 1-3. Chapter 4, in its wilderness historiography, is in fundamental agreement with 5-11, but it is not necessarily a unity since it also contains additions which may be exilic. Deut. 1:34-40, on which 2:14-16 is dependent, lies within two contexts: First, of the spy story of which it is the conclusion, 1:19-46; and second, chapters 1-4. The conclusion of the spy story points to the inclusion of the whole story, which had already

---

[172] Gottfried Seitz, *Redaktionsgeschichtliche Studien zum Deuteronomium,* *BWANT* 13 (Stuttgart: Kohlhammer Verlag, 1971).

[173] Cf. Norbert Lohfink, *Das Hauptgebot: Eine Untersuchung literarischer Einleitungsfragen zu Dtn. 5-11,* (Rome: Instituto Biblico, 1963) and Seitz, *Redaktionsgeschichtliche Studien,* p. 176; some of the conclusions of Seitz in particular seem quite cogent and, although that enquiry lies beyond our present scope, the most relevant of them are noted.

[174] Noth, *Überlieferungsgeschichtliche Studien,* pp. 12, 91, 110.

[175] Cross, *Canaanite Myth,* p. 287.

been told in 9:23, without this conclusion. The secondary and exilic character of 1:19-46 (and 2:14-16), and of the sections of Joshua and Judges which correspond to them, and the sharp contrast to Deut. 1-11 which otherwise is quite consistent in this regard, indicate the existence of a pre-exilic edition (Deuteronomic, Dt), of which the Deuteronomistic history (Dtr) is an exilic expansion with very dramatic modifications. The reasons for these theses are offered below.

The approach employed here begins with the earlier wilderness historiography of Deut. 5-11, on the basis of which 4 and then 1-3 are examined, along with some of the relevant passages of Exodus, Numbers and Joshua—II Kings.

To begin with the obvious, Deuteronomy consists of speeches given by Moses to the people who are about to enter the Promised Land. In part, these speeches introduce the promulgation of the law. The introduction to the promulgation reviews the experiences of the Wilderness and, in light of those experiences, draws didactic conclusions which apply those experiences to the impending occupation of the land. Much can be learned from these speeches concerning the character and identity of those to whom they are addressed.[176]

---

[176] The approach employed here received its initial impetus from Wijngaards' "Dramatization of the Salvific History," p. 48, and also pp. 45, 46, 46n, 47; the same approach was recently adopted, apparently independently, by Seeligmann ("Erkenntnis Gottes und historisches Bewusstsein im alten Israel," in Donner, ed., *Beiträge zur Alttestamentlichen Theologie*, pp. 444-445), who applied it in a more systematic fashion than Wijngaards to Deuteronomy but gives no explanation for his conclusions which, so far as they go, do comport with the results of this essay; and he leaves several outstanding problems unresolved which are broached by his conclusions; relevant here also are the works of Lohfink and Plöger, both of whom offer explanations for certain of the contents of Deuteronomy related to the problems of the wilderness generation which suggests a relation of those contents to political events; but J. G. Plöger, in *Literaturkritische, formgeschichtliche und stilkritische Untersuchungen zum Deuteronium, BBS* 26 (Bonn: Hanstein Verlag, 1967, pp. 53-54, 60, 108), does not sufficiently explore this; nor does Lohfink, "Darstellungskunst und Theologie in Dtn 1, 6-3, 29" (*Biblica* 41, 1969), esp. pp. 133-134, 133n, who suggests a conclusion which, though true, remains unconvincing because of problems which remain unresolved in this particular study; these problems are not resolved by W. L. Moran, "The End of the Unholy War and the Anti-Exodus" (*Biblica* 44, 1963), pp. 333-342; and the outstanding problems are compounded by Lohfink's subsequent essay "Auslegung deuteronomischer Texte IV. Verkündigung des Hauptgebots in der jüngsten Schicht des Deuteronomiums (Dt 4, 1-40)," in *Bibel und Leben* 5 (1964), pp. 247-256; none of the above studies, moreover, correctly relates the Deuteronomic wilderness historiography to that of JE; additional relevant works are cited in the course of this monograph.

By beginning this analysis with the older stratum of chapters 5-11 and 4 of Deut., and proceeding chronologically, a more precise view of the interrelations of the successive sources, and in this case, the relation of Dt to JE, is afforded. Approaching the analysis from Chapter I as it now stands, poses difficulties which require less than satisfactory explanations to resolve them. For example, in Deut. 5:1-3, Moses summons the people and says: "The Lord our God made a covenant with us in Horeb. Not with our fathers did the Lord make this covenant, but with us, who are all of us alive here this day." Reading this in light of Deut. 1:35-40 and Deut. 2:14-16, which have announced the death of the wilderness generation, von Rad writes:

> In view of Deut. 2:14ff., we are surprised by the remark that this covenant was made not with an earlier generation but with those who are now alive. Even though the death of the Sinai generation had occurred meanwhile and lay outside the speaker's view, his intention is clear enough. He wants to bring the event of the covenant making which already belongs to the past vividly before the eyes of his contemporaries.[177]

On the contrary, this is the same generation which left Egypt, journeyed through the Wilderness and is now about to enter the Promised Land. There is ample evidence to support this argument. For example, in chapter 6, Moses tells the audience that when their sons ask them the meaning of the laws and ordinances, they are to answer:

> We were Pharaoh's slaves in Egypt; and the Lord brought us out of Egypt with a mighty hand; and the Lord showed signs and wonders, great and grievous against Egypt and against Pharaoh and all his household, before our eyes. . . And the Lord commanded us to do all these statutes, to fear the Lord our God, for our good always, that he might preserve us alive, as at this day.[178]

In chapter seven Moses reminds them again:

> Remember what the Lord your God did to Phar-

---

[177] Gerhard von Rad, *Deuteronomy: A Commentary, OTL* (Philadelphia: Westminster, 1966), p. 55.

[178] Deut. 6:21-24.

> aoh and to all Egypt; the great trials which your
> eyes saw, the signs, the wonders, the mighty hand
> and the outstretched arm, by which the Lord our
> God brought you out.[179]

This is particularly clear in 11:2-7 where the younger generation is
expressly excluded:

> And consider this day (since I am not speaking to
> your children who have not known or seen it),
> consider the discipline of the Lord, your God, his
> greatness, his mighty hand and his outstretched
> arm, his signs and his deeds which he did in Egypt
> to Pharaoh, the king of Egypt, to their horses and
> to their chariots; how he made the water of the
> Red Sea overflow them as they pursued after you,
> and how the Lord has destroyed them to this day;
> and what he did to you in the wilderness until you
> came to this place; and what he did to Dathan and
> Abirham the sons of Eliab, son of Reuben; how
> the earth opened its mouth and swallowed them
> up, with their households, their tents, and every
> living thing that followed them, in the midst of Is-
> rael; for your eyes have seen all the great works of
> the Lord which he did.[180]

The reference to the "children" is not as Lohfink supposes, purely
rhetorical; rather, the children lend additional emphasis to what the
wilderness generation has "seen."[181] Elsewhere, in Deut. 10:21,
"he is your God, who has done for you these great and terrible
things which your eyes have seen;" from 29:2-3: "You have seen all
that the Lord did before your eyes in the land of Egypt . . .the
great trials which your eyes saw." Chapter 4, or at least part of it, is
in accord with the view that the same generation which left Egypt is
about to enter the land:

> Or has any god ever attempted to go and take a
> nation for himself from the midst of another na-
> tion, by trials, by signs, by wonders, and by war,
> by a mighty hand and an outstretched arm, and
> by great terrors, according to all that the Lord
> your God did for you in Egypt before your eyes?

[179] *Ibid.,* 7:18-91a.

[180] Deut. 11:2-7.

[181] Lohfink, *Das Hauptgebot,* p. 116.

> To you it was shown that you might know that the
> Lord is God.[182]

This usage is consistent throughout the Deuteronomic wilderness historiography. The same generation which came out of Egypt is about to enter the Promised Land. This accords with JE.[183]

The audience is composed of the remnant of those who left Egypt, not the entire contingent. But it is not an innocent remnant. Opponents of this view might argue that since Dt expressly notes that the nation had been in the Wilderness for forty years, the wilderness generation has already died off. But this would require the imputation to Dt of the subsequent usage in Dtr, meanings which are radically different.

Mention of the exact forty years' duration of the Wilderness occurs three times in Deut. proper, twice in chapter 8 and once in chapter 29:

> You have seen all that the Lord did before your
> eyes in the land of Egypt . . . the great trials
> which your eyes saw, the signs, and those great
> wonders; but to this day the Lord has not given
> you a mind to understand, or eyes to see, or ears
> to hear. I have led you forty years in the Wilderness; your clothes have not worn out upon you,
> and your sandals have not worn off your feet.[184]

This precise legal significance of the forty years duration is more important in the subsequent Deuteronomistic historiography, but it is also of significance in the Deuteronomic and should be clarified here. It is, in the words of Noth, " . . .in the Old Testament, the life span, within which a man participates in the life of the community with full powers and rights."[185] In other words, this includes

---

[182] Deut. 4:34-35.

[183] This confirmation of the JE scheme by Deut., coupled with the lack of contrary evidence in JE, renders unacceptable the opinions of De Vries ("The Origin of the Murmuring Tradition," *JBL* 87, 1968, p. 58) and D. Sackenfeld ("The Problem of Divine Forgiveness in Numbers 14," *CBQ* 37, 1975, p. 322) that J had recounted the demise in the wilderness of the generation which left Egypt; for a similar view see North, *Old Testament Interpretation of History,* p. 31.

[184] Deut. 29:2-5.

[185] Noth, *Numbers,* p. 110.

not only legal rights and duties, but military responsibilities as well. This forty-year term applies to males between age 20 and age 60. The "children" mentioned in the text, are those between 5 and 20; the "little ones" from birth to five years.[186] Although losing their full legal rights and duties at 60, the people are still accorded recognition, being valued at a bit less than one-third of an adult male between 20 and 60.

As previously noted, the references to the forty-year Wilderness duration in Amos are probably Deuteronomic additions. The dramatic embellishments of the Wilderness are as much in evidence here as they are in pre-exilic Prophecy. It is the "great and terrible wilderness, with its fiery serpents and scorpions and thirsty ground where there was no water."[187] Chronologically, of course, the forty-year period is a fiction. Von Rad rightly observes that "how and where Israel had spent this long time, our narrator cannot indeed describe clearly to the reader, any more than can his earlier predecessors . . . the relevant traditional material is completely insufficient to fill up this period adequately."[188]

In Dt as in pre-exilic prophecy, the Wilderness, along with the other great saving acts, is, in and of itself, a source of the obligation of the nation to obey God. But in Dt another highly significant dimension is added:

> And you shall remember all the way which the Lord your God has led you these forty years in the wilderness, that he might humble you, testing you to know what was in your heart, whether you would keep his commandments, or not. And he humbled you and let you hunger and fed you with manna, which you did not know, nor did your fathers know; that he might make you know that man does not live by bread alone, but that man lives by everything that proceeds out of the mouth of the Lord. Your clothing did not wear out upon you and your foot did not swell, these forty years.[189]

Here the great saving acts, the Wilderness among them, consti-

---

[186] See Lev. 27: 1-8.

[187] Deut. 8:15; also 29: 2-6; for this see Weinfeld, *Deuteronomy.*

[188] von Rad, *Deuteronomy,* p. 42.

[189] Deut. 8:2-4.

tute not only an obligation, but are part of the preface to the new covenant. They are recited as a part of the new covenant which is to be made here in Moab on the border of the Promised Land. It is identical in structure to the Sinaitic covenant which was based on those same saving acts, to which are now added those which have occurred between Sinai and Moab. The embellished Wilderness and its miraculous forty-year duration are part of the prolegomena of the new covenant, the covenant "which the Lord commanded Moses to make with the people of Israel in the land of Moab, besides the covenant which he had made with them at Horeb."[190] Chapters 5-11 are the prolegomena, 12-26 the terms of the covenants; 27 (28) and 29 contain the blessings and curses. This has long been recognized.

The forty-year duration in Dt thus has a retributive dimension related directly to the new covenant. It offers a period of testing and humbling to determine whether or not the people will obey the covenant. The miracle of the manna is mentioned as proof of the Lord's omnipotence, but a more specifically didactic dimension is added in Dt: It was given that "he might make you know that man does not live by bread alone."[191] The effect of the whole Dt theology expressed in its wilderness historiography is to show man's utter dependence on God and thereby to stress the need for obedience.

But the people did not acquit themselves well during this period of testing and humbling; rather, they showed themselves to be evil: "Remember and do not forget how you provoked the Lord our God to wrath in the wilderness,"[192] an assessment the same as that of JE. It is based on the incidents of rebellion in the Wilderness recorded in JE, and is evaluated in terms of the JE scheme of retribution. But while J is content merely to portray and allow the reader to draw his own conclusion, Dt renders the conclusion in the form of a summary judgment: "From the day you came out of the land of Egypt, until you came to this place, you have been rebellious against the Lord."[193] And even more condemning: "You have been

[190] *Ibid.,* 29:1.

[191] Deut. 8:3.

[192] *Ibid.,* 9:7a.

[193] *Ibid.,* 9:7b; for this and for the composition of chapter 9 in general, cf. Lohfink, *Das Hauptgebot,* pp. 217, 219; and Seitz, *Redaktionsgeschichtliche Studien,* pp. 56, 57, 91.

rebellious against the Lord from the day I knew you."[194] Various instances of rebellion are adduced as evidence: Moses warns the people not to "put the Lord our God to the test, as you tested him at Massah."[195] Elsewhere he reminds them: "At Tab'erah also, and at Massah, and at Kib'roth-hatta-avah, you provoked the Lord to wrath. And when the Lord sent you from Ka'desh-bar'nea, saying, 'Go up and take possession of the land which I have given you' then you rebelled against the commandment of the Lord our God, and did not believe him or obey his voice."[196] Several features in this sequence are noteworthy as supporting the judgment that "you have been rebellious against the Lord from the day I knew you." The incident at Massah, from Exod. 17, is the third instance of murmuring in the Wilderness, but it occurs before the Sinaitic covenant. In Deut. 6:16, this incident is given as an example of putting God "to the test." In the more severe theology of Deuteronomy, although the people are not yet legally bound by the covenant, any example of faithlessness is reprehensible. Massah is mentioned again in Deut. 9:22-23, along with the rebellions in the Wilderness which occurred at Tab'erah and Kib'roth-hatta'avah. All three "provoked the Lord to wrath." Although the people were punished in the other two instances, both of which are post-Sinaitic, they were not punished at Massah, which is pre-Sinaitic.

The mention of the spy episode at Ka'desh'bar'nea is of the utmost importance. It is given as an example of rebelliousness, and presumably punishment, but no more is said of it. The Ka'desh'bar'nea spy-story is the episode from Num. 14 in which the people sinned by failing to obey the Lord's commandment to occupy the land. This sin was punished in J by the curse that none who "despised" the Lord would see the land.

In chapter 4:3-4 the incident at Ba'al-pe'or is mentioned, including the punishment. Those who followed Ba'al were "destroyed from among you, but you who held fast to the Lord your God are all alive to this day".

The abominable behavior of the people in the Wilderness, and the consequences of their actions, are emphasized in the review of the events at Horeb, particularly the apostasy of the Golden Calf.

[194] Deut. 9:24.

[195] *Ibid.*, 6:16.

[196] *Ibid.*, 9:22-23.

Deut. 9 does not mention the punishment of the plague which is contained in JE. However, it does offer a considerably expanded version of that incident. In this version, which may belong to Dt or may be part of the later Dtr redaction, but which is in fact compatible with both, the Lord intended, for their apostasy, "to destroy them and blot out their name from under heaven."[197] This destruction does not occur, however, because Moses intercedes. He does not plead that the people do not merit annihilation, since he admits that they are wicked, but presents a manifestly contrived argument for why they should not be destroyed, namely, that the Egyptians will hear of it and will say: "Because the Lord was not able to bring them into the land which he promised them, and because he hated them, he has brought them out to slay them in the Wilderness."[198]

By this device the rectitude of the ultimate punishment is affirmed in principle but is averted in practice. To render the configuration consistent, this novel explanation is integrated into the JE account in two places: Exod. 32:11-14 and Num. 14:13-19. We accept the view of von Rad that the relevant passages in Exod. 32 were taken from Deut. 9.[199] By virtue of this incorporation into JE, the more severe standard of Dt is extended to the earlier tradition. The consistency of the new configuration is maintained by the simultaneous explanation of the failure to execute the sentence. The consistency does not require that punishment be inflicted, but makes only the assertion that it was deserved.

Other additions find their way into the three pre-Sinaitic murmuring episodes, in the form of censures and admonitions, as, for instance, in Exod. 15:25b-26; Exod. 16:4b; and Exod. 17:2b.[200]

The conclusion to be drawn from the foregoing is that despite the evil nature of the wilderness generation, this generation will inherit the Promised Land. The land is of seminal importance in Deutero-

[197] Deut. 9:13.

[198] *Ibid.*, 9:28.

[199] von Rad, *Deuteronomy,* p. 79; for opinions as to whether Exodus 32:7-20 is Deuteronomic or Deuteronomistic, cf. Coats, *Rebellion,* pp. 186-188 (Dtr.); Noth, *Exodus,* p. 225 (Dtr); Seitz, *Redaktionsgeschichtliche Studien,* pp. 58-64 (Dt. with expansion).

[200] These have been attributed both to Deuteronomic and Deuteronomistic editors; they certainly belong to one or the other but there is no decisive evidence; Noth, *Überlieferungsgeschichtliche Studien,* p. 32, n. 9; Childs, *Exodus,* p. 266; Coats, *Rebellion,* pp. 55, 83-84; Zenger, *Sinaitheophanie,* p. 164.

nomic theology, which, in fact, outlines the conditions that determine the possession of the land, especially given the extreme losses accumulated by the end of the seventh century. The relation between loyalty to God and the possession of the land, already expressed in JE, is brought into much sharper focus in Deuteronomy. The latter uses the JE explanation for the original possession and subsequent loss of the land. It is that loss which caused the Deuteronomic theology to scrutinize the conditions of its initial possession. Those conditions are embodied in the JE wilderness archetype which portrays *the beginning* of the land's possession. This point will be summarized below.

Dt, in the main, applies not only the JE system of retribution, but relies on the facts interpreted in that system. As shown, Dt does enhance the severity of the JE system by reinterpreting some of its facts and by stating conclusions drawn from them in summary form. In the matter of the relation of sin and possession of the land, Dt is similar to JE. In the earlier sources the remnant of those who left Egypt enters the land, but it is not a righteous remnant. Rather, it consists of those who have escaped punishment in the JE system. Due to the collective nature of obligation in JE, the punishment of some is the punishment of all. Consequently, many of the guilty individuls were not punished although collective punishment was inflicted in post-Sinaitic instance of rebellion. Dt sustains the JE estimate of the wilderness generation: "From the day you came out of the land of Egypt, until you came to this place, you have been rebellious against the Lord." But this estimate is incompatible with the political disasters that transpired since the writing of JE, including the loss of much land, a loss which is attributed to sinfulness. It can be inferred that the Deuteronomic theologians were acutely aware of this inconsistency by the several explanations they offer for the initial possession of the land by that sinful generation.

Not all of the wilderness generation is about to possess the land, either in JE or in Dt. Possession is open only to those who have survived the punishments inflicted on that generation. This view is implied in Dt which refers to those punishments as examples of provoking the Lord's wrath. Dt expressly records that those who sinned at Ba'al-pe'or were punished by death: "But you who held fast to the Lord your God are all alive this day."[201] The contingent

---

[201] Deut. 4:4.

which is about to make the new covenant at Moab is composed of survivors of the Wilderness. Dt states that they are sinful, and clearly implies that only some of the sinful have been punished by the Lord's wrath along the way. Dt makes this explicit regarding Ba'al-pe'or and in the Moab incident there is a clear connection between those who are guilty and those who are punished. In other examples mentioned in Dt, such a connection is not clear. Moreover, all, including this remnant addressed by Moses, sinned at Sinai with the Golden Calf.

The justifications for the land's acquisition by this sinful generation are not given systematically but four distinct reasons are given to render the retributive system consistent. First, acquisition is viewed as a result of the Promise to the Patriarchs. The deliverance from Egypt and gift of the land are effected by God, "because He loved your fathers."[202] He is bringing them into "the land which he swore to give to your fathers."[203] Thus, in one sense, the Promise to the Patriarchs remains unconditional; the land is a gift to the nation in its corporate capacity, but it is by no means an unconditional gift to all the individuals who comprise the nation. The same element of conditionality introduced by J with the covenant exists here, and becomes clearer when the other reasons for the land's acquisition are examined. The second reason can be found in the following passage:

> Do not say in your heart, after the Lord your God has thrust them out before you. It is because . . . of my righteousness that the Lord has brought me in to possess this land; whereas it is because of the wickedness of these nations that the Lord is driving them out before you. Not because of your righteousness or the uprightness of your heart are you going to possess their land; but because of the wickedness of these nations, the Lord your God is driving them out before you, and that he may confirm the word which the Lord swore to your fathers, to Abraham, to Isaac, and to Jacob.
>
> Know, therefore, that the Lord your God is not giving you this good land to possess because of

---

[202] *Ibid.*, 4:37-38; 6:10.

[203] *Ibid.*, 7:8; 6:23.

> your righteousness; for you are a stubborn people.[204]

By means of this device of evaluating the previous inhabitants, a thoroughly novel factor is introduced. Yet it is artificial because the Canaanites have no relation to Jahweh and no obligation to obey Him.[205] The introduction of a novel element into the archetype radically modifies the composition of that archetype. All the components are now placed in different relations to each other. By virtue of this modification, the authority of the archetype, within the historical configuration of which it is the determinate paradigm, is reasserted. By configuration is meant the entire range of relevant variables that extend chronologically, from the archetype through the evolving present. The archetype does not determine exactly what its own modifications will be, but it does provide the categories (in this case, the system of retribution) through which those modifications will be effected when necessary. Due to the static character of the categories in the archetype, *i. e.,* the retributive structure, the individual variables of both the archetype and its configuration, necessarily modify to sustain the consistency of the entire configuration over time. The dramatic inclusion of the Canaanite variable with the archetype, in terms of its categories, sustains the consistency and precludes the possibility that God rewards sin at one time and punishes it at another, a possiblity that would render reality both unjust and unintelligible by virtue of its mutability. The Promise to the Patriarchs and sinfulness of the Canaanites explain how the sinful remnant of a sinful generation can occupy the land.

Events, and especially significant events, do not occur by accident in Dt. They are integrated into the retributive system and evaluated in terms of it. For example, the fact that Moses did not enter the Promised Land is "probably one of the oldest features of the Mosaic tradition."[206] But in Dt this is shown to be a result of divine order. As a punishment for the sins committed by the people, God orders Moses not to enter the Promised Land: "The Lord was angry with me on your account, and He swore that I should not cross

---

[204] Deut. 9:4-6.

[205] This may also be a part of the Deuteronomic message to its contemporaries who have adopted the Canaanite practices and who are losing the land as a consequence of that adoption.

[206] Noth, *Numbers,* pp. 213-215.

the Jordan.''[207] Given a consistent theological significance in Dt, which may have added it, or by Dtr in which it certainly occurs,[208] this explanation for God's judgment against Moses modifies the older tradition, and in doing so constitutes the third reason why the sinful generation can enter the land.

The fourth reason given by Dt for the gift of the Promised Land to the sinful generation is the new covenant. The relation of the Deuteronomic covenant, which is made just before the entrance into the Promised Land, and the Sinaitic covenant, is a very complicated subject and we shall no more than touch upon the relevant aspect of it here.[209] There is evidence that the Deuteronomic covenant, to some degree, supersedes the Sinaitic covenant, and thereby absolves the Wilderness Generation from its sins. This is highly problematic. That this new covenant is made with the generation which came out of Egypt is clear from chapter 29:

> These are the words of the covenant which the Lord commanded to Moses to make with the people of Israel in the land of Moab, besides the covenant which he had made with them at Horeb.
> "And Moses summoned all Israel and said to them: 'You have seen all that the Lord did before your eyes in the land of Egypt . . . but to this day the Lord has not given you a mind to understand, or eyes to see, or ears to hear. I have led you forty years in the Wilderness; . . . that you may know that I am the Lord your God . . . Therefore be careful to do the words of this covenant, that you may prosper in all that you do.
> 'You stand this day all of you before the Lord your God; the heads of your tribes, your elders, and your officers, all the men of Israel, your little ones, your wives . . . that you may enter into the sworn covenant of the Lord your God, which the Lord your God makes with you this day; that he may establish you this day as his people, and that he may be your God, as he promised you, and as he swore to your fathers, to Abraham, to Isaac and to Jacob. Nor is it with you only that I make this sworn covenant, but with him who is not here

[207] Deut. 4:21; also 31:2-3; 34:5.

[208] Cf. Noth, *Numbers,* pp. 213-215.

[209] Perlitt, *Bundestheologie,* pp. 64, 68, 81, 99, 100, 101; von Rad, *Old Testament Theology,* I, pp. 220-221.

> with us this day as well as him who stands here
> with us this day before the Lord our God.[210]
>
> 'You have declared this day concerning the
> Lord that he is your God, and that you will walk
> in his ways, and keep his statutes, and his com-
> mandments and his ordinances, and will obey his
> voice; and the Lord has declared this day concern-
> ing you that you are a people for his own posses-
> sion, as he has promised you.' ''[211]

By virtue of this new covenant the wilderness sins of the generation are no longer sins. They have not yet made a covenant, and are
not yet responsible. In chapter 12 Moses cautions them not to do
"according to all that we are doing here this day, every man doing
whatever is right in his own eyes, for you have not as yet come to
the rest which the Lord your God gives you."[212]

But this explanation is inconsistent. Throughout the speech Moses has been denouncing the people for their rebelliousness in the
Wilderness. Now they are absolved because they did not understand the significance of the great saving acts. This is inconsistent
with the J account from Exod. 14:31, that "Israel saw the great
works which the Lord did against the Egyptians, and the people
feared the Lord; and they believed in the Lord and in His servant
Moses." It is also inconsistent with the Dt account of the making of
the Moab covenant where Moses commands:

> Take this book of the law, and put it by the side of
> the ark of the covenant of the Lord your God,
> that it may be there for a witness against you. For
> I know how rebellious and stubborn you are; be-
> hold, while I am yet alive with you, today you
> have been rebellious against the Lord; how much
> more after my death![213]

Nevertheless, the intention of the contrived explanation is clear; it
exonerates the sinful generation, enabling it to enter the Promised
Land which is a reward for faithfulness.

---

[210] Deut. 29: 1-15; the usages of the phrase "until this day" in Deut. are interpreted by Brevard S. Childs, in "A Study of the Formula 'Until this Day'," *JBL* 82
(1963), p. 292.

[211] Deut. 26: 17-18.

[212] *Ibid.,* 12:8-9.

[213] *Ibid.,* 31:26, 27.

Hence, there are four justifications given in Dt for the reward of the land to the sinful generation: the Promise to the Patriarchs, the sins of the Canaanites, the punishment of Moses, and the new covenant. To these may be added a fifth: the episodes in which God spares the wicked generation for the sake of His own reputation (Exod. 32:11-14; Num. 14:13-19; Deut. 9:28). These five justifications are obviously contrived but they are necessary for Dt to harmonize the sinful record of the wilderness generation contained in the account which Dt received, with the gift of the land to that same generation. The account of that sinful generation was not received from the prophets but rather from JE, and the JE account presents great problems for the Dt theologians. In that earlier account, sins are apparently rewarded by the bestowal of the land, but at a later time the same sins are punished by the loss of land. The contrived explanations are responses to this problem. Authorities, such as Schmid and Rendtorff, who have argued that J (and E) is the creation of Deuteronomic circles must explain why these circles created such obvious difficulties for themselves, difficulties which they then had to overcome with contrived explanations.[214] If the Dt theologians had relied on the prophetic estimate of the Wilderness, these problems would not have existed. Instead, they disregarded the prophetic account. They relied on the JE account and in light of the problems this posed, it is clear that they did not write that same account. Therefore, JE is not the creation of Dt but rather the source of that later theology.

The contingency of the possession of the land is stressed repeatedly. In connection with the covenant, and a formal part of it, Moses enumerates the blessings for its fulfillment and the curses for its violation. The blessings are peace, plenty and continued possession of the land.[215] It should be observed, at least parenthetically, that these are material rewards for the observance of the physical and material restraints which are enjoined by the covenant; this is an important factor in the evolution of Old Testament spirituality. The Deuteronomic theology reflects a dramatic increase in the severity of the demands of God on man, greatly circumscribing the sphere of free action. And the punishments threatened for trans-

---

[214] Schmid, *Der Sogenannte Jahwist,* pp. 117-118, 166; Rendtorff, *Überlieferungsgeschichtliches Problem des Pentateuch,* pp. 163-64, 75-79, 171.

[215] Deut. 28: 1-4.

gression reflect a correspondingly increased severity. The curses are much more extensive and comprise the bulk of chapters 27-31. The curses, which are lurid in their details, have been expanded by various additions, some of which are clearly exilic.[216] All manner of punishments are predicted in the form of curses, war, deprivation, political defeats, destruction and dispersion. For our present purpose, it is unnecessary to explore these in detail. Since the curses, just as the rest of Deuteronomy, stem from the late seventh and early sixth centuries, they reproduce, in the form of predictions of Moses, the disasters which befell the nation to that later time. By virtue of its fictional accuracy, the authority of the tradition is enhanced. The political disasters are attributed to the breach of the covenant, and are thus the divine punishments for sin. While they differ in magnitude from the punishments in JE, the structure of the Dt system of retribution is identical to that of JE, interpreting the events which have transpired from JE to its own time. The Dt historiography accepts both the retributive structure of JE and the facts recorded by JE in that structure. The Dt awareness of the inconsistency of the sinful generation inheriting the Promised Land, in fact even surviving the Wilderness, is shown by the several explanations for this apparent anomaly, explanations which are not quite consistent but whose purpose is clear enough. In the late seventh century the nation was still in possession of some of the land, despite its continued sinfulness. This situation, although reprehensible and perilous, corresponds to the Dt wilderness historiography which allowed that sinful generation to inherit the land. Some of its elements tend toward the absolution of the guilt of that generation, and since these are so obvious and contrived, they reveal an acute awareness on the part of the Dt theologians of the contradictions in the retributive system, contradictions engendered by the interaction of the received JE record and experience subsequent to it.

The books of Joshua and Judges recount the entrance of the nation into the Promised Land after the death of Moses, and they continue the Deuteronomic history which begins with Deuteronomy and continues through II Kings. The character and identity of pre-Deuteronomic sources in Joshua and Judges has been much disputed. This problem is indeed related to our problem but it is a subject too vast and complicated to be addressed meaningfully

[216] von Rad, *Deuteronomy,* 183.

here.[217] It is generally agreed that there are different Deuteronomic strata in Joshua-Judges but whether these represent major and minor supplements to a basic Dt edition or distinct editions remains problematic.[218] From the vantage of the subject of this essay there are two Deuteronomic editions in Joshua which, because of their radically different wilderness historiographies, can be readily distinguished and explained.

It is sufficient here, following Weinfeld, simply to refer to the earlier elements in Joshua and Judges as "pre-Deuteronomic."[219]

In the pre-Deuteronomic sources the Conquest is undertaken by the same generation which left Egypt, journeyed through the Wilderness and made the covenant at Moab. They are now under the leadership of Joshua. There is no evidence which controverts this and there is evidence which supports it.[220] In chapter 5 the Lord orders Joshua to circumcise the people, which he does.[221]

In the pre-Deuteronomic sources the conquest is more a tribal than a national affair. It is not completed, at least in terms of the previous extent of the land promised to the patriarchs. The Israelites are not powerful enough to conquer all the inhabitants. Some of those who are conquered are not put to the ban, in accord with the divine command, but are left to dwell among the Israelites or to do forced labor for them. The failure to conquer all the land is regarded as a sin in the pre-Deuteronomic sources. Moreover, the Israelites worship foreign gods during the conquest under Joshua.[222] The non-expulsion of the inhabitants, which is directly related to the ensuing apostasy, is related causally to the defeats of the Israelites during the period of the Judges which are explained by the "sin

[217] Cf. for example, M. Noth, *Das Buch Joshua, HAT* (2nd ed; Tübingen: Mohr, 1953), p. 16; S. Mowinckel, *Tetrateuch, Pentateuch, Hextateuch, BZAW* 20 (1964); O. Eissfeldt, *The Old Testament,* p. 256; Artur Weiser, *The Old Testament: Its Formation and Development* (NY: Association Press, 1961), pp. 143-147.

[218] Cf. Noth, *Das Buch Joshua,* pp. 9-10; J. Wenham, "The Deuteronomic Theology of the Book of Joshua," *JBL* 90 (1971), p. 140.

[219] See his "The Period of the Conquest and of the Judges as seen by the Earlier and Later Sources," *VT* XVII (1967), pp. 93-113.

[220] Jos. 24:6-7, 16-17; but compare Noth, *Joshua,* pp. 137-138.

[221] *Ibid.,* 5:2-3,8.

[222] For all of the above see M. Weinfeld, "The Period of the Conquest," pp. 94-97, 102, 105-106.

of not driving out the Canaanites."[223]

The Dt edition of the pre-Deuteronomic sources effects radical changes in those sources. It writes its own account to show that, in the words of Weinfeld:

> Joshua had put the entire population of Canaan to the ban in compliance with the law of the ban in Deut. XX, 16-17 . . . There were, consequently, no grounds on which the Israelites could be accused of not driving out the Canaanites who dwelled among them. On the other hand, however, the Deuteronomist did confess that Canaanites continued to dwell on the periphery of the Israelites' settlement, i. e., that Canaanites still remained within the *ideal* territory did not constitute a sin in the Deuteronomist view because Joshua had driven out the people of Canaan as God had commanded.[224]

Dt makes a sharp theological distinction between the period of Joshua and that of the Judges. The former is "depicted as a golden age in which the Israelites worship only Jahweh and ony with the passing of Joshua's generation do the Israelites begin to do evil in the sight of the Lord. The period of the judges is here stamped entirely with the imprint of sin and rebellion."[225]

Since the wilderness generation is perfect under Joshua, at least so far as its behavior in the land is concerned, there can be no reason for its inability to conquer all the land. This inconsistency is rectified by a modification of the word of God which attributes the inability to conquer to the divine plan; the remaining peoples must "test" the Israelites of the coming generations. If the latter do not follow them in their religions, they will be able to conquer the remainder of the land. "And since the oncoming generations have not stood the test, the remaining land has been forfeited forever."[226]

Different generations do figure in this Dt account of the conquest, and they figure in it theologically, but not completely. This

---

[223] *Ibid.,* p. 100; Weinfeld has meticulously developed a cogent argument whose conclusion comports with the one first suggested by Eissfeldt in his *The Old Testament,* p. 255; see also Noth, *Überlieferungsgeschichtliche Studien,* p. 21.

[224] Weinfeld, "Conquest," pp. 100-101.

[225] *Ibid.,* p. 105.

[226] *Ibid.,* p. 102.

generation "served the Lord all the days of Joshua, and all the days of the elders who outlived Joshua, who had seen all the great works which the Lord had done for Israel."[227] All that generation died and there followed it another "who did not know the Lord or the work which he had done for Israel."[228] It is here that the significance of the references in Deuteronomy to the children who have not witnessed the saving acts becomes apparent. The author who admonishes the generation which has seen them to relate them to their children who have not seen them, is the same author who recounts the degeneration of those children in the land after the demise of the wilderness generation. Although Dt makes a sharp distinction between these generations which occupy the land, it does not make any distinctions between generations which enter the land. True, the generation of Moses and Joshua does serve the Lord "all the days of Joshua," but before it crossed the Jordan, as Moses said in Deut. 9, "from the day you came out of the land of Egypt, until you came to this place, you have been rebellious against the Lord."[229] It is this same generation which, however wicked it was in the Wilderness, is perfectly faithful in the Promised Land. Apparently its evil acts in the Wilderness are nullified by the Dt covenant at Moab, and the particular elements in that covenant already described.

Dt does recognize that children have been born in the Wilderness. It adds to the circumcision ceremony of the pre-Deuteronomic sources in Josh. 5 the explanation that this ceremony is a second circumcision. The first took place before the people came out of Egypt; the second is for those born in the Wilderness.[230]

The Dt historiography of the Wilderness and Conquest is theologically consistent, and it sustains this consistency by continued reconstructions. But the message to its seventh-century audience is clear: Just as the wilderness generation was able to overcome its earlier wickedness and take possession of the land, so will its seventh century descendants be able to retain the land if they observe the law.

In conjunction with the didactic intention of its historiography,

[227] Judg. 2:7.
[228] *Ibid.,* 2:10.
[229] Deut. 9:7.
[230] Jos. 5:2,5.

Dt modifies the JE system of collective retribution. According to JE, the sins of the fathers are visited upon the children "to the third and fourth generation."[231] By contrast, Dt asserts the principle of individual retribution: Each is punished for his own sins without regard for the sins of his ancestors. Weinfeld has opined that the older sources were modified to accord with this view[232] but he has not satisfactorily explained this modification or observed its inconsistencies, although he does note that the principle parallels a similar concept in wisdom literature. The reason for the change is that if the nation is being punished for the sins of its ancestors, then no degree of faithfulness can avert its destruction and all Deuteronomic exhortations are rendered nugatory.

In this Dt historiography the land has become a factor of paramount importance. Its possession is the sole sign of divine favor or disfavor and is based on the fulfillment or non-fulfillment of the covenant.[233]

Ps. 78 differs radically from the psalms previously considered. It displays in full measure the wickedness of the people in the Wilderness, and their continued apostasy in the land. Although in the facts of the Exodus and Wilderness which it recounts it parallels JE, its intensification of the wickedness of these facts is very similar to the intensification in Dt. It recounts in great detail how the nation rebelled in the Wilderness, and how it was punished repeatedly, although not to the point of destruction.

> Their heart was not steadfast
> towards him;
> They were not true to his
> covenant.
> Yet he, being compassionate,
> forgave their iniquity,
> and did not destroy them;
> he restrained his anger often,
> and did not stir up all his
> wrath.[234]

[231] Deut. 5:9-10; Exod. 20: 5-6; also Jer. 31:30; 32:17-19.

[232] See Weinfeld, *Deuteronomy,* pp. 316-319.

[233] See for example, Wijngaard's "Salvific History", p. 37; von Rad, "The Promised Land and Yahweh's Land in the Hextateuch," *Problem of the Hextateuch,* pp. 90-91.

[234] Ps. 78:37-38.

The psalm continues from its account of the Wilderness to re-count the fall of the Northern Kingdom which "turned away and acted treacherously like their fathers . . . moved him to jealousy with their graven images." For this the Lord punished them by al-lowing them to be conquered: While "he rejected the tent of Jo-seph . . . he chose the tribe of Judah."[235]

Dahood suggests[236] that the psalm's composition dates from 922-721, but given the historical content, this seems improbable. Weiser notes the affinity with Deuteronomy but cautions that simi-larities may be derived from a common source rather than direct imitation.[237] He also sees in the psalm a historiography similar to that in Amos, Hosea and Jeremiah. This view is unacceptable since the wilderness historiography of the psalm and those of these prophets diverge radically. Rather, it appears to be a product of the late pre-exilic period.

The Deuteronomic interpolations into Jeremiah reflect that his-toriography of the wilderness generation which supersedes the esti-mate of the period of pre-exilic prophecy. For example, in contrast to Jeremiah's own view, "I remember the devotion of your youth, your love as a bride, how you followed me in the wilderness,"[238] ac-cording to the Deuteronomic addition to Jer. 7:

> For in the day that I brought them out of the land of Egypt . . . they did not obey or incline their ear but walked in their own counsels and the stub-bornness of their own hearts and went backward and not forward. From the days that your fathers came out of the land of Egypt to this day, I have persistently sent all my servants the prophets to them, day after day, yet they did not listen to me, or incline their ear but stiffened their neck. They did worse than their fathers.[239]

---

[235] Ps. 78:67-68.

[236] Dahood, *Psalms,* II, p. 238, and compare: David Noel Freedman, "Divine Names and Titles in Early Hebrew Poetry," in Frank Moore Cross, et al., eds., *Magnalia Dei: The Mighty Acts of God: Essays on the Bible and Archeology in Memory of G. Ernest Wright* (NY: Doubleday, 1976), pp. 78-82.

[237] *The Psalms,* pp. 539-40.

[238] Jer. 2:2a.

[239] Jer. 7:22-26; cf. W. Thiel, *Die Deuteronomistische Redaktion von Jeremiah,* 1-25, *WMANT* 41 (Neukirchen Vluyn: Neukirchner, 1973), pp. 121-125.

8: The Deuteronomistic (Dtr) Wilderness Historiography

Although there are examples in the Deuteronomistic history of individual punishments for individual sins, the system of collective responsibility is employed in that work to explain the fall of Jerusalem to the Babylonians.[240] In II Kings that explanation is:

> Because Manasseh, king of Judah, has committed these abominations and has done things more wicked than all the Amorites did, who were before him, and has made Judah also to sin with his idols; therefore says the Lord, the God of Israel . . . I will wipe Jerusalem as one wipes a dish wiping it and turning it upside down. And I will cast off the remnant of my heritage and give them into the hands of their enemies, and they shall become a prey and a spoil to all their enemies, because they have done what is evil in my sight and have provoked me to anger since the day their fathers came out of Egypt, even to this day.[241]

Despite the dramatic reforms of King Josiah, "still the Lord did

[240] See von Rad, "The Deuteronomic Theology of History in I and II Kings," in *Problem of the Hextateuch,* pp. 205-221; Weinfeld, *Deuteronomy,* pp. 15-27.

[241] 2 Kgs., 21:10-15.

not turn from the fierceness of his great wrath by which his anger was kindled against Judah, because of all the provocations with which Manasseh has provoked him."[242] Freedman rightly notes that this is a "forced attempt to explain why Josiah failed."[243]

It is clear from this that the system of collective retribution prevails in Dtr. There, the entire nation, guilty and innocent, is permanently punished because of the sins of one king, Manasseh. Here the king represents the nation in its corporate capacity.

This punishment might in part have been explained by cumulative guilt, but from the modifications effected by Dtr. in Dt and JE, it is clear that this explanation was thought inadequate. The loss of much of the land had broached the question of the conditions of its original acquisition, and for Dt this had neceessitated a reinterpretation of its acquisition, which was done as indicated above. The loss of all the land broached the same question again, and occasioned an additional reinterpretation of its acquisition.

The Dtr wilderness historiography which embodies this reinterpretation manifests itself in parts of Deut. 1-3 and in Joshua. The first three chapters of Deuteronomy recount certain events of the Wilderness and Conquest of the land east of the Jordan. Among these is the episode at Kadeshbarnea, recounted by J, where the people rebel against the divine command to begin the conquest of the land. As a result of this rebellion, Dtr says:

> And the Lord heard your words, and He was angered, and He swore, "Not one of these men of this evil generation shall see the good land which I swore to give to your fathers, except Caleb, the son of Jephun'neh; he shall see it, and to him and to his children, I will give the land upon which he has trodden, because he has wholly followed the Lord." The Lord was angry with me also on your account, and said, "You also shall not go in there; Joshua, the son of Nun, who stands before you, he shall enter; encourage him, for he shall cause Israel to inherit it. Moreover, your little ones, who you said would become a prey, and your children who this day have no knowledge of good or evil, shall go in there and to them I will give it, and they shall possess it. But as for you,

[242] *Ibid.,* 23:26-27; also 24:3, 18-20.

[243] Freedman, "Deuteronomic History," *IDB Supp.,* p. 227.

> turn, and journey into the wilderness in the direction of the Red Sea.[244]

The same punishment of the generation occurs in chapter 2:

> And the time from our leaving Kadeshbarnea until we crossed the brook Zered was thirty-eight years, until the entire generation, that is, the men of war, had perished from the camp, as the Lord had sworn to them. For indeed, the hand of the Lord was against them, to destroy them from the camp until they had perished.[245]

The same punishment is added to the conquest account in Joshua. Here we follow Noth's analysis of the sequence of sources but supply our own conclusions as to the significance of that analysis. The primary or pre-Deuteronomic elements are given in capitals, the first supplement in standard type, and the second supplement italicized. The first supplement belongs to Dt, the second to Dtr:

> AT THAT TIME THE LORD SAID TO JOSHUA, "MAKE FLINT KNIVES AND CIRCUMCISE THE PEOPLE OF ISRAEL AGAIN THE SECOND TIME." SO JOSHUA MADE FLINT KNIVES AND CIRCUMCISED THE PEOPLE OF ISRAEL AT GIBEATH-HAARALOTH. *And this is the reason why Joshua circumcised them; all the males of the people who came out of Egypt, all of the men of war, had died on the way in the wilderness after they had come out of Egypt.* Though all the people who came out had been circumcised, yet all the people that were born on the way in the wilderness after they had come out of Egypt had not been circumcised. *For the people of Israel walked forty years in the wilderness, till all the nation, the men of war that came forth out of Egypt, perished, because they did not hearken to the voice of the Lord; to them the Lord swore that he would not let them see the land which the Lord had sworn to their fathers to give us, a land flowing with milk and honey. So it was their children, whom he raised up in their stead, that Joshua circumcised, for they were un-*

---

[244] Deut. 1:34-40.

[245] *Ibid.*, 2:14-15.

circumcised, because they had not been circumcis-
ed on the way.[246]

No exhaustive analysis of the stages of composition of Deut. 1-3 (4) is offered here; this is far beyond the scope of our present concern. The curse of the wilderness generation in Dtr is clearly subsequent to the historiography of that generation in Dt, irrespective of the stages by which that curse was added to its immediate context of Deut. 1-3, and the stages of composition of that context itself. Few, if any, authorities would deny this, however much their reconstructions of Deut. 1-3 (4) may diverge.[247]

Plöger's conclusion that 1:20-46 (with the possible exception of 1:41-46 which may date even later) is a unified addition, seems correct. Additional weight is lent to this by von Rad who stresses the

[246] *Joshua,* 5:2-7; see Noth, *Das Buch Joshua,* pp. 9,23; Soggin does not note the theological importance of this modification, observing only that "none of this, however, provides a satisfactory answer to the question why the generation who travelled through the wilderness could not have been circumcised"; see his *Joshua: A Commentary,* p. 71; Robert G. Boling does note that the event is both anomolous and contrived but does not explain this; see his *Joshua: A New Translation with Notes and Commentary* (AB; NY: Doubleday, 1982), pp. 187-189, 193-194.

[247] Lohfink ("Darstellungskunst"); and Plöger (*Deuteronomium,* pp. 51, 52-53, 210) both note its place in the system of theological retribution; moreover, both suggest a connection between the curse and the exile, but neither offers an explanation for this; the more recent reconstruction of Mittman is problematic; he includes in the "Grundschicht" of Deut. 1:1-6,3, elements of 1:34, 1:39 and 1:40, which are constituent components of the generation curse, but relegates to a later stage the inclusion of 2:7, which clearly regards the forty-year duration as a blessing and not as a punishment and thus, in our view, belongs to the earlier Dt stage; he may well be correct in regarding certain elements of the generation curse as additions, but these elements, while they do clarify it, do not constitute it; moreover, he attributes certain of these to P and this should remain an open question, but only regarding the clarifying additions, not the constituent components of the curse. See Siegfried Mittmann, *Deuteronomium 1:1-6,3; Literarkritisch und traditionsgeschichtlich untersucht,* BZAW 129 (Berlin: De Gruyter, 1975), pp. 37, 56, 57, 61, 72, 78, 119-173.

In view of the several references in Deut. 4 which indicate that the first wilderness generation has seen all the great saving acts and is about to enter the land, the view of Lohfink, in "Auslegung deuteronomischer Texte IV, Verkündigung des Hauptgebots in der jüngsten Schicht des Deuteronomium (Dt. 4, 1-40)" (*Bibel und Leben,* 5, 1964, pp. 247-256), that Deut. 4 is the latest addition to the Dtr corpus, which he regards as early exilic, cannot be accepted; for a similar view of 4:1-40, see Freedman ("The Deuteronomic History," p. 226); in light of our own conclusion an analysis of Deut. 1-4 in terms of these elements we have noted we do share Freedman's view that 1-3 are pre-exilic; as regards 4:1-40, our present research has produced no evidence that it is not a unity, or even that it is not a secondary insertion, but it is not the last addition to the Dtr corpus; compare: George Braulik, *Die Mittel Deuteronomischer Rhetorik: Erhoben aus Deuteronomium, 4, 1-40, An Bib* 68 (Rome: Biblical Institute Press, 1978, and in particular pp. 78-81; A. D. H. Mayes, "Deuteronomy 4 and the Literary Criticism of Deuteronomy," *JBL* 100 (1981), pp. 24, 30-31.

sequence of the account.[248] The spy episode at Kadeshbarnea had already been noted as an instance of rebellion in Deut. 9:23 which, despite its brevity, follows JE. In Deut. 1, the story is recounted again, now with drastic consequences: The wilderness generation is punished by death. This extreme punishment is anticipated by the Dtr modification of the *sequence* of the account, and by certain additions to that sequence. In the J account Moses sends spies to observe the land. They report that it is a good land, but that the inhabitants are strong and the cities well fortified. Moses urges them to occupy it but the people refuse, wanting to return to Egypt. As punishment for their lack of faith, none who "despised" the Lord will see the land.[249] In the Dtr account, the spies report that it is a good land. But the people rebel immediately, even before any mention is made of the strength of the inhabitants.[250] Their sinfulness is further increased by Moses' exhortation that the Lord will fight for them "just as He did for you in Egypt before your eyes, and in the wilderness, where you have seen how the Lord your God bore you, as a man bears his son, and all the way that you went until you have come to this place."[251] The intent of this intensification of wickedness is clear, and it appears to anticipate the greater Dtr punishment with which the episode concludes: The annihilation of the wilderness generation. Questionable is the view of Lohfink that the speech of Moses in Deut. 1:29-34 replaces the speech of Moses in Num. 14:11-22.[252] These speeches complement each other; the latter explains why the punishment was not executed immediately, the former records its execution.[253] Moreover, the speech in Numbers is part of the prophecy-fullfillment scheme so characteristic of Deuteronomic historiography. In the Dtr addition to Numbers the punishment is stated and its fullfilment predicted: "None of the men

---

[248] Plöger, *Deuteronomium*, pp. 41, 44; von Rad, *Deuteronomy, p. 41;* Plöger does note that 2:14-15 is out of place in the "Weg und Kampfbericht (11,13) but follows W. L. Moran in his "The End of the Unholy War and the Anti-Exodus," *Biblica* (1963), p. 342.

[249] Num. 13:18-20, 22-24, 27-31, 14:4-11, 23b.

[250] Deut. 1:25-26.

[251] *Ibid.,* 1:30-31.

[252] Lohfink, "Darstellungskunst."

[253] Also questionable is Lohfink's view that 3:1-3 continues 2:24-31 and these are the "Gegenbild" to Deuteronomy 1; that is their present sequence, but their original sequence was the opposite ("Darstellungskunst," p. 130).

who have seen my glory and my signs which I wrought in Egypt and in the Wilderness, and yet have put me to the proof these ten times and have not hearkened to my voice, shall see the land which I swore to give to their fathers."[254] The fullfilment of this prediction is recorded in Deut. 2:14, "as the Lord had sworn to them."

The various characterizations of those who are punished, "these men of this evil generation," "the entire generation" and "the men of war," are consistent and all denote men between the ages of 20 and 60, ages of military service which correspond to the ages of full legal rights and duties.[255]

By virtue of this dramatic modification of the Dt usage of the forty-year Wilderness duration as a blessing (evident not only in Deut. 1:7, indicating that this, and its immediate context, belong to an earlier edition of the history), Dtr converts that same duration into a punishment.

As Lohfink and Plöger have suggested, this radically different wilderness historiography is connected with the exile. The destruction of Jerusalem and exile of the year 587 were not only catastrophic but *unprecedented.* For the first time since the Conquest *all* the land was lost and the state ceased to exist.[256]

By virtue of its unprecedented character, and in light of the traditions which prevented it from being interpreted because of its magnitude, the catastrophe remained unintelligible. The Dtr modifications indicate that its authors regarded the explanation for the land's acquisition in JE and Dt as inadequate when viewed in the light of the land's loss. The earlier historiography could not solve the problem posed by divine leniency at the land's acquisition and severity regarding its loss. Thus the conditions of the land's possession are rendered chaotic and consequently unintelligible. The successive modifications which we have traced are attributable to the persistence of the categories of the JE historiography which, in light of subsequent events, necessitated modifications of some of the details of that same JE historiography. The JE account, in its facts and its interpretations, is the basis of the subsequent accounts

---

[254] Num. 14:22-23a.

[255] But see Mittman, *Deuteronomium,* pp. 69, 72.

[256] For this see M. Noth, "The Jerusalem Catastrophe of 587 B. C. and its Significance for Israel," *The Laws in the Pentateuch and other Studies* (Philadelphia: Fortress, 1967), pp. 260-280.

which render the wilderness archetype theologically consistent with the evolving events of the configuration explained paradigmaticaly by that archetype.

By this dramatic modification of both the JE and Dt historiographies, the entire wilderness generation is annihilated. Those who enter the Promised Land are members of the perfect generation, those who "have no knowledge of good or evil" and are comparable in goodness to Adam and Eve before the Fall. Because of this modification, the inconsistency in the earlier accounts represented by the entrance of the evil generation into the good land is removed. The Dt account had already addressed this problem in terms of generations and had resolved it by making the conquest coextensive with the life of the wilderness generation, exonerating that generation and portraying it as perfectly faithful during the conquest period. But the same Dt account had intensified the wickedness of that generation during its stay in the Wilderness. The incongruity remained in the Dt account, of a wicked generation, whose wickedness was intensified because it had witnessed the great saving acts, inheriting the Promised Land. In light of this, the loss of all the land and exile are both unprecedented and unintelligible because of the magnitude of punishment they represent. After all, the sins of Manasseh are pale beside those of the wilderness generation, evil since Moses knew it, which had seen the saving acts with their own eyes.

By including the curse of the wilderness generation, and thereby dramatically modifying the wilderness archetype, the theological consistency of that archetype with the subsequent configuration, that now includes the loss of all the land, is reasserted. God is shown to act consistently, exacting similar punishments for similar sins at different times. Not only the justice but also the intelligibility of the history is preserved. The determinants of the historical phenomena are rendered timeless and thus immutable. By this the intelligibility of the phenomena is sustained. Two interrelated aspects of this problem, however, must be considered. The Dtr historiography looks not only to the past but to the future. Both Lohfink and Plöger have suggested some connection of this severe punishment of the wilderness generation with the exile.[257] This connection deserves to be examined.

[257] Plöger, *Deuteronomium,* pp. 51-52, 202-203; Lohfink, "Darstellungskunst," pp., 133-134.

The loss of all the land is not only rendered intelligible, but the conditions for the reacquisition of the land are provided as well.[258] According to this analysis, there is an expectation of a return in Dtr. The land is of paramount importance in Dtr, but in light of its loss it is theologically more important still. What Dtr asks of the exiles is not merely obedience, but innocence comparable to that of the generation which first possessed the land. The ultimate result of the JE theology and the subsequent events which it interprets, is the total subordination of man to God, primeval innocence, unattainable in light of men's seemingly ineradicable sinfulness, or destruction. Still, it is a material reward, the land, which is offered for the complete renunciation of the physical and material self which the severe standard demands.

Considerations of a more theoretical nature concerning the interactions of the historiographies and the character of Old Testament historiography in general will be discussed following a brief consideration of the wilderness historiographies of exilic Prophecy, P, and the Psalms.

---

[258] Noth denied that Dtr held out any hope for the future but subsequent studies have demonstrated that various expectations are contained in Dtr; Cf. H. W. Wolff, "The Kerygma of the Deuteronomic Historical Work," *Vitality of Old Testament Traditions*, pp. 24-100; von Rad, *Old Testament Theology*, I, pp. 334-347; Lohfink, "Bilanz nach der Katastrophe—Das Deuteronomistische Geschichtswerk," *Wort und Botschaft*, p. 207; A. Soggin, "Deuteronomistische Geschichtsauslegung während des babylonischen Exils," in F. Christ, ed., *Oikonomica: Heilsgeschichte als Thema der Theologie: Oscar Cullmann zum 65. Geburtstag gewidmet* (Hamburg: Reich, 1967), pp. 14-15; Lohfink, "Auslegung deuteronomistischer Texte"; W. Brueggemann, "The Kerygma of the Deuteronomistic Historian," *Interpretation* 22 (1968); Cross, *Canaanite Myth*, p. 288; H. K. Krause, "Gesetz und Geschichte," *Evangelische Theologie* 11 (1951-52), p. 427.

9: The Wilderness Historiography of P

Some scholars have argued recently that P dates from either before D (and Dtr) or is contemporary with it. These views notwithstanding, the prevailing consensus maintains that P comes later than D and Dtr. However, the possibility that P is contemporary with the latter should remain open.[259] Both Dtr and P, however, are clearly exilic, as unified literary sources, irrespective of pre-literary evolution.

P's concern is predominantly cultic but some of its content is directly related to the retributive aspects of the wilderness period.[260]

In addition to supplying precise chronologies and genealogies, P makes certain substantive contributions to the wilderness historiog-

---

[259] Cf. Cross, *Myth,* pp. 307, 324-325; Weinfeld, "Period of the Conquest and Judges"; and his *Deuteronomy,* pp. 179, 95n; R. Killian, "Die Priesterschaft—Hoffnung auf Heimkehr," *Wort und Botschaft,* p. 230; K. Elliger, "Sinn und Ursprung der priesterlichen Geschichtserzählung," *ZTK* 49 (1952), pp. 142-143; Weiser, *The Old Testament,* p. 138; Otto Kaiser, *Introduction to the Old Testament,* pp. 103-104, 107-109; Volkmar Fritz, *Tempel und Zelt; Studien zum Tempelbau und zu dem Zeitheiligtum der Priesterschaft, WMANT* 47 (Neukirchen-Vluyn: Neukirchner, 1977), pp. 1-2.

[260] For the historical dimension of P's cultic concerns see: C. Westermann, "Die Herrlichkeit Gottes in der Priesterschaft," *Forschung im Alten Testament* (München: Kaiser, 1974), pp. 128-133.

raphies of the earlier sources. P replaces the second murmuring episode of J in Exod. 16, which is pre-Sinaitic, with its own, stating that on the fifteenth day of the second month after leaving Egypt, the people murmur against both Moses and Aaron.[261] Since the J account cannot be determined, the P modification is left open as well. The interpretation of the murmuring differs, however, in that it is regarded not as a rebellion against Moses and Aaron but against God. "Your murmurings are not against us but against the Lord."[262] In this passage, the seriousness of the murmuring is enhanced. The consequences are similar to those of the J account, although the details are elaborated and a cultic-commemorative significance is added: "Let an omer of it be kept throughout your generation, that they may see the bread with which I fed you in the wilderness, when I brought you out of the land of Egypt."[263] In addition, P notes that the people ate manna for forty years in the Wilderness. Although the duration is given, no reason for that specific amount of time is yet offered.[264] P adds no punishment for this pre-Sinaitic murmuring and thus sustains the JE retributive system.

The Lord orders Moses to take a census of the people in the Wilderness at Sinai, "every male head by head; from twenty years old upward, all in Israel who are able to go forth to war."[265] This command occurs in the second month of the second year after the people had come out of Egypt.

The major contribution of P to the Wilderness narrative occurs in the spy episode at Kadeshbarnea.[266] Given all the literary sources contained in this episode, which describes the first approach to the land, it is of decisive significance. In the P account, God orders Moses to send men to spy out the land. P's account is very detailed, going so far as to name the spies. They spy the land for forty days, return with some of its fruit, but bring back "an evil report of the land," describing it as a "land that devours its inhabitants" and

---

[261] Exod. 16:1-3.

[262] *Ibid.,* 16:8

[263] *Ibid.,* 16:32

[264] *Ibid.,* 16:35a.

[265] Num. 1:1-3.

[266] See for this S. E. McEvenue, *The Narrative Style of the Priestly Writer, AnBib,* 50 (Rome: Biblical Institute Press, 1971), pp. 90-144.

populated by "men of great stature" who, by comparison, made
the spies seem like grasshoppers.[267]

The people are terrified: "Would that we had died in the land of
Egypt! Or would that we had died in this wilderness! . . . would it
not be better for us to go back to Egypt?"[268] Joshua and Caleb, two
of the spies, exhort them and warn them not "to rebel against the
Lord." The spies, except for Joshua and Caleb, are killed immediately by a plague,[269] but the rest of the congregation is punished in a
different way:

> Your dead bodies shall fall in this wilderness; and
> all of your number, numbered from twenty years
> old and upward, who have murmured against me,
> not one shall come into the land where I swore
> that I would make you dwell except Caleb the son
> of Jephun'neh and Joshua the son of Nun. But
> your little ones who you said would become a
> prey, I will bring in, and they shall know the land
> which you have despised. But as for you, your
> dead bodies shall fall in this wilderness. And your
> children shall be shepherds in the wilderness forty
> years, and shall suffer for your faithlessness; until
> the last of your dead bodies lies in the wilderness.
> According to the number of the days in which you
> spied out of the land, forty days, for every day a
> year, you shall bear your iniquity, forty years, and
> you shall know my displeasure. I, the Lord, have
> spoken; surely, this will I do to all this wicked
> congregation that are gathered together against
> me: in this wilderness they shall come to a full
> end, and there they shall die.[270]

The P punishment of the wilderness generation closely resembles
that of Dtr; yet there are differences. Although the forty years is a
punishment in both and brings about the same result, in P the duration is based upon the number of days for which the land was spied.
In Dtr the forty years in the Wilderness are counted from Egypt
and are related to the signs and wonders which that generation (legally) witnessed. It is from Egypt that the post-Sinaitic obligation
to obey begins in Dtr. But in P, which does not mention Egypt, the

[267] Num. 13:25-26; 13:32-33.

[268] *Ibid.,* 14:1-3.

[269] *Ibid.,* 14:36-38.

[270] *Ibid.,* 14:26-35.

forty years appear to be counted from the taking of the census right after the events at Sinai. P records in Deut. 1:3 that Moses addressed the people in Horeb, at the end of the Wilderness, "in the fortieth year." This represents the forty years from Sinai (or Kadesh-barnea), while in Dtr the thirty-eight years is given for the duration of this period.

These divergencies are relatively minor. Fundamentally the P punishment of the wilderness generation accords with that of Dtr, and both differ radically from Dt and JE.

Other passages dealing with the annihilation of the wilderness generation occur in Num. 6:62-65 and Num. 32:6-15. These passages are more problematic and Noth attributes them to "revisions in the Dtr spirit" or to insertions made in order to harmonize the Tetrateuch and Deuteronomic history when these two works were joined together.[271]

In the Dtr account the inability of Moses to enter the Promised Land is interpreted as a punishment even though the sin is vague: "The Lord was angry with me on your account."[272] In P this punishment is attributed to a particular sin, " . . . because you did not believe in me, and sanctify me in the eyes of the people of Israel."[273] Here Moses himself is held responsible.

P adds Korah to Dathan and Abiram of J who rebel against the leadership of Moses. In conjunction with the increasing severity of the punishments, the Lord orders Moses and Aaron to separate themselves from the congregation "that I may consume them in a moment." Moses intercedes, and the rebels are punished as in the J account.[274]

Thus despite P's great concern with cultic matters, it does not lack an important retributive dimension which emphasizes the necessity for obedience and gives its own rendition of the consequences ensuing from disobedience. The lessons of P's wilderness historiography, like those of Dtr, are intended for an exilic[275] audience and contain both the hope and the conditions of return.

[271] See Noth, *Numbers,* pp. 9, 204, 210, 213-214, 235-238.

[272] Deut. 3:26; 4:2; 31:2; 31:14.

[273] Num. 20:12; 27:12-14.

[274] *Ibid.,* 16:1-5, 16-25, 31-35; it is significant for the relative dates of Dt and P that while Deut. 11:6 mentions Dathan and Abiram, it does not mention Korah.

[275] For P's expectations see Kilian, "Die Priesterschaft, *Wort und Botschaft,* p. 231; Cross, *Canaanite Myth,* p. 325; Noth, *Pentateuchal Traditions,* p. 243.

10: The Wilderness Historiography of Ezekiel and Exilic Psalms

With a few variations, the wilderness historiography of Ezekiel is similar to that of Dtr. Ezekiel does not mention a forty-year duration, but in his account there are two generations in the Wilderness, and they are equally wicked.[276] Because of its disobedience the first generation is punished by not being able to enter the land.[277] Their children are ordered, also in the Wilderness, not to follow the example of their fathers. "Nevertheless the children rebelled against me."[278] This second generation also merited annihilation, but the Lord withheld that punishment for the sake of His name. Instead, the Lord swears that the people will be scattered among the nations.[279]

It is clear that the account of Ezekiel lacks the almost mathematical precision of Dt, Dtr and P. Different generations exist but these

[276] Ezek. 20:1-26.

[277] *Ibid.,* 20:15.

[278] *Ibid.*

[279] For this see Walther Zimmerli, *Ezekiel: A Commentary on Chapters 1-24* (Philadelphia: Fortress Press, 1979), p. 481.

do not correspond to the generations of the other accounts nor to their retributive systems. In Ezekiel one evil generation follows another and the exile is attributed to the punishment of the children of the first wilderness generation. There is no good generation, nor are there explanations as to why the children, who are as wicked as their fathers, are able to enter the land—other than the fact that the Lord sustains His purpose for His own sake.

Ezekiel relies not only on Pentateuchal sources but on older sources. For example, in his account the people worshipped other gods even in Egypt, despite the Lord's command that those gods must be abandoned.[280] A trace of this account is found in the pre-Deuteronomic strata of Joshua in 24:14-15, where the people deserved destruction. But there as in the Wilderness, this punishment was not inflicted because the Lord "acted for the sake of my name, that it should not be profaned in the sight of the nations among whom they dwelt."[281] Of all the wilderness historiographies, Ezekiel's is the most negative. He employs a device also used by Dt, portraying the Lord as restraining His anger for His own sake in Egypt, the Wilderness and in the land, even when the people merit destruction.

Despite all these difficulties, Ezekiel uses the Wilderness as a paradigm for the future repossession of the land:

> I will bring you out from the people and gather
> you out of the countries where you are scattered
> with a mighty hand and I will bring you into the
> Wilderness of the land of Egypt, so I will enter in-
> to judgment with you, says the Lord God. I will
> make you pass under the rod, and I will let you go
> in by number. I will purge out the rebels from
> among you, and those who transgress against me.
> I will bring them out of the land where they so-
> journ but they shall not enter the land of Israel.[282]

Here there is a contrast between the new occupation, which is to be selective, and the first occupation which was not. Two distinct systems of retribution, collective and individual, correspond to each occupation. On the one hand, the nation has received a collective punishment with the exile, on the other the individuals are to answer for themselves before the new Wilderness and new occupa-

---

[280] Ezek. 20:7-8; 23:8.

[281] *Ibid.,* 20:9.

[282] *Ibid.,* 20:34-38.

tion. Although these two conceptions are placed in tension in Ezekiel, his book contains one of the clearest and most unconditional statements of individual retribution: "The soul that sins shall die. The son shall not suffer for the iniquity of the father, nor the father suffer for the iniquity of the son; the righteousness of the righteous shall be upon himself, and the wickedness of the wicked shall be upon himself."[283]

Although Ezekiel clearly relies on elements in the Pentateuchal sources, including Dt and Dtr, he fashions them for use in his own way. The variations in Ezekiel may, in large part, be attributed to the spontaneous character of prophetic utterance, a style which contrasts sharply with the analytical histories of the Pentateuchal theologians. While the former reflects the evolving tradition of the latter, it does not do so with exactitude. However much Ezekiel varies from the Pentateuchal sources, both remain diametrically opposed to the wilderness historiography of pre-exilic Prophecy.

Pss. 95 and 106, with minor variations, express the wilderness historiography of Dtr. Both are exilic. The wilderness content of 95 is not extensive but is significant in that it states: " . . . for forty years I loathed that generation . . . therefore I swore in my anger that they should not enter my rest."[284] Ps. 95 mentions the murmurings at Massah and Meribah, but makes no mention of Kadesh-barnea. These references are used as examples of putting "me to the proof, though they had seen my work."

Ps. 106 contains the most extensive wilderness historiography in the Psalter. Like Ezekiel it begins the rebellion of the wilderness generation with the murmuring of the people as they are being pursued by the Egyptians before the miracle at the Red Sea, an incident in Exod. 14:10-14, which is J. It is noteworthy that this incident is never cited as an instance of rebellion in Deuteronomic historiography. Now that the annihilation of the wilderness generation has entered the tradition, its wickedness is extended to other elements of the archetype. Any doubt, whether before Sinai or even before the Red Sea, is now regarded as rebellion. Since the generation is to be annihilated, its wickedness is enhanced by attributing to it new instances of rebellion, no matter when they occur. The psalm does not follow the Pentateuchal sequence but rather selects episodes

---

[283] Ibid., 18:20.
[284] Ps. 95:8-11.

from it: The "wanton craving" for meat from the J episode in Num. 11; the rebellion against Moses and Aaron of Dathan and Abiram (with no mention of Korah) from the J account in Num. 16; and the apostasy of the Golden Calf, including the Deuteronomic interpolations. It also mentions the apostasy of Ba'al-Pe'or and the rebellion at the waters of Meribah. Concerning the spy episode, the psalm relates the same consequence as Dtr: The Lord "raised his hand and swore to them that He would make them fall in the wilderness".[285] As does Ezekiel, the psalm appears to attribute the destruction and exile to the wickedness of the wilderness generation, interpreting the admonitions of Dtr, which conditionally attribute the exile to disobedience, as unconditional punishments in the forms of curses that are fulfilled by the exile. On the other hand, the psalm also records that the apostasy of the people following the occupation of the land provoked the Lord's anger, precipitating the subsequent destruction. Except for minor variations, and a few omissions, the psalm follows the historiography of Dtr. The psalm is exilic.[286]

In the view of Weiser, "there can be no question of a direct literary dependence by the Psalm on the Pentateuch; both of them seem to originate in a common cultic liturgical tradition."[287] While this question should remain open, the psalm's dependence on the Pentateuch, and on the Dt and Dtr histories, appears probable.

[285] Ps. 106:26; the account of the Ba'al-Pe'or episode in Ps. 106 differs both from JE and from Hosea; see Mendenhall, *The Tenth Generation,* p. 106.

[286] Dahood, *The Psalms,* pp. 3, 76; thus, problematic is the view of Weiser that is is not necessarily exilic and that parts of it which seem exilic "can just as well be understood to refer to a calamity that has come upon the people, for instance, after the destruction of the Northern Kingdom," *Psalms,* p. 681.

[287] *Ibid.,* p. 681.

11: Summary

The Jahwist wilderness historiography contains a consistent system of divine retribution in which the Sinai covenant occupies a position of decisive importance. In this system of retributive theology, the unconditional promise of the land to the patriarchs is rendered conditional, dependent on the fulfillment of the covenant. While the structure of J's retributive theology is both clear and consistent, the details of its constituent punishments are problematic. Employing the principle of collective responsibility, the punishment of some members of the nation by God in J is a punishment of the entire nation. Consequently, those members of the wilderness generation who reach the Promised Land are not the innocent remnant but rather those who have survived the collective punishments in the Wilderness, in which all have been punished by the symbolic punishment of some.

The J wilderness historiography is an archetype. It explains how the land came to be possessed and the conditions of that possession in terms of its retributive theology. It also explains the continued possession of the land to J's own time, not by abstract discussion but by a paradigmatic portrayal in the wilderness archetype. More important, by virtue of its retributive dimension the J Wilderness historiography is the archetype of divine justice in the history of Israel. The archetype contains not only the facts relevant to that theme, but the categories within which these facts are interpreted and from which they derive their significance in the retributive scheme. J's work is not a mere chronicle. Its proper intention is not only explanatory but, related to that, also didactic, although its didactic purpose is somewhat problematic.

Notwithstanding the fragmentary and problematic character of the Elohist elements in the JE wilderness historiography, to the extent that it can be determined, E conforms to the retributive structure of the covenant theology of J.

Pre-exilic Prophecy does not base the obligation of the nation to obey God on the Sinaitic covenant, but rather on the great saving acts, which are magnified and thus rendered even more miraculous. The estimate of the wilderness generation in pre-exilic Prophecy is positive. It regards that generation as faithful, and in this it differs radically from the JE account. Hosea is the exception in his clear emphasis on the covenant. In contrast, the pre-exilic prophets regard the nation as obligated by those great saving acts and as subject to the punishment of the loss of the land for sinfulness. They employ, with some exceptions, a collective system of retribution and threaten the loss of the land for the sins of some of the people.

The JE wilderness historiography is the source of the pre-exilic Deuteronomic wilderness historiography. Arising in the seventh century when much of the land had been lost and the remainder endangered, and when apostasy seemed almost ineradicable, it interpreted these phenomena in terms of the JE retributive theology and the latter's close causal connection between loyalty and reward, sin and punishment, made manifest by losses of the Promised Land and continuing apostasy. The Dt interpretation of the simultaneous phenomena of apostasy and the loss of land which, within the framework of the JE theology, had portrayed these two elements in close causal relation, is the theological matrix of the Dt theology. The apparent confirmation of JE by subsequent events imparted to JE an unparalleled authority. That enhanced authority of JE, indeed *thoroughly vindicated authority of JE,* in conjunction with the perilous possession of the remaining land, is the source of the characteristic intensity of Deuteronomic theology. Its hortatory style and fundamentalism are attributable at least as much to its conviction as to its (problematic) institutional sources. Moreover, its evident exasperation was undoubtedly engendered and sustained by the obliviousness of the nation to which its truths were preached —an unconcern which, to the Deuteronomists, must have seemed suicidal.

Deuteronomic theology draws from prophecy its dramatized portrayal of the dangers of the Wilderness, thereby magnifying the guilt of the generation. Nevertheless, it relies on JE for its portrayal of the wilderness generation. Dt stresses in those dramatizations the witnessing of the great saving acts from Egypt onward by that generation. In light of these factors, the behavior of the wilderness generation appears even worse than in the JE account. This is a wicked generation, wicked since the day Moses knew it; yet this generation had entered the Promised Land. The Dt objective was not to display the rewards for sin and apostasy, however, and it effected modifications which render the wickedness of that generation consistent with its possession of the land. It expands the wilderness archetype to include the initial possession of the land and it renders that modified archetype, by the infusion of novel elements and contrived explanations, theologically consistent in terms of retribution. Among these are its relative goodness in comparison with the previous inhabitants, and its perfect faithfulness under Joshua. These justifications for the gift of the land to the sinful generation are cogent proof that the JE theology is not the creation of the Deuteronomic theologians. The older account of the Conquest is modified and subordinated to the need for theological consistency in terms of the retributive dimension of the theology. Thus the JE wilderness archetype, which provides the structure and the events in terms of which the experiences of Dt are interpreted, is modified by Dt to yield an archetypal explanantion consistent with those new experiences. By means of these modifications, the JE archetype is expanded so that the conditions of the land's continued occupation and partial loss are rendered consistent with the explanation for its initial occupation. Thus the JE archetype retains its authority to explain the relevant facts from the beginning to the present, but because the Dt past and present differ from the JE past and present, the need for configurational consistency necessitates modifications. The modifications are determined by the interaction of the JE archetype and subsequent events. Such modifications are effected by expansions, interpretations and interpolations, all within categories of the JE archetype of retribution. Dt's theology stresses individual responsibility in its retributive system, although not consistently. These modifications are reflected in the relevant Psalms we have considered.

The exilic Deuteronomistic wilderness historiography effects further modifications in the wilderness archetype of Dt, which had dramatized the wickedness of the wilderness generation but which had introduced considerations that explained its acquisition of the land despite that wickedness. In light of the loss of all of the land, attributable to the apostasy of people and kings, the extenuating circumstances introduced by Dt to explain the land's occupation by the wicked generation were superseded by the Dtr archetype which annihilates the wilderness generation and substitutes a new, completely innocent generation. This is effected by employing an exact component of the Dt archetype, the forty-year duration, and radically reinterpreting it as a punishment instead of a blessing as one of the miraculous acts in the salvation sequence. This modification is also effected in terms of the JE retributive categories which retain their authority throughout the sequence while some of the events of the JE account undergo modification to render them consistent with subsequent events interpreted in terms of these categories. The P wilderness historiography, with possible minor variations, is identical in this respect to Dtr. Ezekiel and the exilic Psalms, with some variations, reflect the basic exilic Dtr Pentateuchal wilderness historiography. This salient and dramatic modification required but slight changes for the conquest period since the Dt historiography had already so modified the pre-Deuteronomic sources as to render the people faithful in that period. Dtr further fictionalized it by the simple substitution of one generation for another. By the forfeiture of *all* the land by *all* the wilderness generation, the Dtr wilderness archetype now also explains the later loss of *all* the land by *all* the nation. Hence, precedents for all relevant subsequent events of the configuration are at this point expressed in the Dtr wilderness archetype. Destruction and exile are rendered intelligible by their paradigmatic portrayal in the past in the archetypical wilderness historiography. God does not act with leniency regarding the nation at one point in time, and with severity at another, rendering propitiation uncertain or even impossible, reality chaotic and thus unintelligible. On the contrary, with regard to the land, God acts with complete consistency, and the explanation for His actions, and thus for reality, is contained in the archetype. As new experiences are incorporated into the evolving configuration, by providing the framework within which they are interpreted, the archetype to some degree determines its own modifications. Some facts of JE, along with the categories within which all the JE facts were interpreted, persist throughout the sequence. These remain constant, and only because they remain constant do they necessitate the modification of other aspects of the original JE archetype so that the archetype is made to express exact precedents for the evolving events of the configuration explained by the archetype. Although Dt effects changes in the retributive system which tend toward individual retribution, Dtr reasserts the principle of collective responsibility. Only in Ezekiel does individual retribution emerge with clarity, although collective responsibility is still in evidence.

Until the exile, the possession of the land, which represented peace and material prosperity, especially in comparison with Egyptian servitude, was the visible expression of divine favor or disfavor. However, the land was a corporate possession of the nation and while it lasted, the system of collective retribution persisted, although with modifications. Only when it was lost did man as an individual stand accountable before God. The inquiry gradually shifts to the individual as an independent moral entity, obligated, as before, to obey the divine law, but now subject as an individual to the consequences of obedience and disobedience. A complex but profound evolution of the notions of sin, punishment and reward, collective and individual responsibility is visible in the sequence under examination, an evolution which has not been systematically explored here. The clear tendency is toward increasing severity of the standard and, concomitantly, an increasing spirituality which accords material and physical indulgence but reluctant and slight recognition. Material deprivation may still be regarded as a punishment, but material reward is in tension with the spirituality which is demanded for it. Formulated with consistency, virtue thus becomes its own reward; this standard applied to history manifests itself as apocalyptic eschatology which offers an extra-terrestrial spiritual reward for virtue which is coupled with a physical punishment for sin. But the previous historical-theological tradition regarding the land is the retributive tradition from which apocalyptic eschatology ultimately emerges as the inquiry into the good, evil and justice of the individual, by the scrutiny of the record of the world from the first manifestation of these phenomena. Thus with the loss of the land and emergence of the individual, the historiographical focus of Old Testament theology shifts to the appropriate and more comprehensive archetype, the origin of good and evil—also the creation of J.

12: Reconsideration of Myth and History

It is a commonplace of Old Testament scholarship, that ancient Israel, in contrast to the neighboring peoples, with the advent of her historical consciousness made a radical departure from the mythic view of reality. In contrast to that mythic ontology which expresses a reality that is cyclical, essentially timeless, thus immutable and constituted forever by primordial events archetypically expressed, Israel came to express her reality in history, as a linear sequence of irreversible, unrepeatable unique events, in a temporal sequence.[288] The various works of Mircea Eliade contain some of

---

[288] A. Malamat, "The Doctrine of Causality in Hittite and Biblical Historiography," *VT* 5 (1955); E. A. Speiser, "Ancient Mesopotamia," in R. Dentan, ed., *The Idea of History in the Ancient Near East* (New Haven: Yale University Press, 1955), p. 60; H. Cancick, *Grundzüge der Hetheitischen und Alttestamentlichen Geschichtsschreibung und Historische Wahrheit, SBS* 48 (Stuttgart: Katholisches Bibelwerk, 1970); Eva Osswald, "Alt-orientalische Parallelen zur Deuteronomistischen Geschichtsschreibung" *MIO* 15 (1969); L. Clapham, "Mythopoetic Antecedents of the Biblical World-View and their Transformation in Early Israelite Thought," in Cross, ed., *Magnalia Dei;* J. J. M. Roberts, "Myth Versus History," *CBQ* 38 (1976); B. Albrektsen, *History and the Gods;* W. G. Lambert, *Babylonian Wisdom Literature* (Oxford: Clarendon Press, 1960), pp. 63-91; James B. Pritchard (ed.), *Ancient Near Eastern Texts Relating to the Old Testament* (3rd ed.; Princeton: Princeton University Press, 1969), pp. 227-568, *passim.*

the most lucid and forceful expressions of this inveterate distinction. For example:

> Judaism presents an innovation of the first importance. For Judaism, time has a beginning and it will have an end. The idea of cyclical time is left behind. Yahweh no longer manifests himself in cosmic time like the gods of the other religions, but in historical time which is irreverisble. Each new manifestation of Yahweh in history is no longer reducible to an earlier manifestation. The fall of Jerusalem expresses Yahweh's wrath against his people but it is no longer the same wrath that Yahweh expressed by the fall of Samaria.[289]

The research presented in this paper does not sustain this sharp distinction between myth and history. The religion of ancient Israel is expressed in the history of ancient Israel and that history is its expression of reality. Its ontology is not expressed at one time or in abstract form.[290] Von Rad has noted that "we can only describe the Old Testament's revelation of Yahweh as a number of distinct and heterogenous revelatory acts."[291] But the emphasis on this relativism and its corresponding linearity has tended to ignore the operation of constants and persistence in the process. The revelations are distinct and heterogenous only to a degree and only on the phenom-

---

[289] Mircea Eliade, *Sacred and Profane* (NY: Harper and Row, 1959), pp. iii, 92, 111; and his *Myth and Reality* (NY: Harper and Row, 1963), p. 140, and *Myth of the Eternal Return* (Princeton: Princeton University Press, 1954), pp. 11, 104, 107, 14, 141; for similar views: M. Noth, "Die Historisierung des Mythos im Alten Testament," *Gesammelte Studien* (München: Kaiser, 1957), pp. 31-32, 47; E. A. Speiser, "The Biblical Idea of History in its Common Near Eastern Setting," *Israel Exploration Journal* 7 (1957), pp. 207-208; Simon de Vries, *Yesterday, Today, and Tomorrow: Time and History in the Old Testament* (London: S. P. C. K., 1975), pp. 39, 281-282, 342-349; W. Pannenberg, "Redemptive Event and History," in Westermann, *Essays in Old Testament Hermeneutics,* p. 316; Millar Burrows, "Ancient Israel," in Robert Dentan, ed., *The Idea of History in the Ancient Near East,* pp. 127-128; Brevard Childs, *Memory and Tradition in Israel, SBT MS* (Naperville: Allenson, 1972), pp. 82-84; Henri Frankfort, *Intellectual Adventure of Ancient Man* (Chicago: University of Chicago Press, 1946), "Introduction"; for a somewhat different view cf. R. Smend, *Elemente alttestamentlichen Geschichtsdenkens, TS* 92 (Zürich: EVZ, 1968), pp. 10-15; and Manfred Weippert, "Fragen des israelitischen Geschichtsbewusstseins," *VT* 22 (1973), pp. 428, 435, 441; Paul Ricoeur, *The Symbolism of Evil* (Boston: Beacon, 1967), p. 5.

[290] Compare Hartmut Gese, "Erwägungen zur Einheit der biblischen Theologie," *ZTK* 67 (1970).

[291] von Rad, *Old Testament Theology,* pp. 1, 115.

enal level. The same is true of the alleged uniqueness and irreversibility of the events. For example, although the wilderness historiographies do not express absolute primordial reality, they do express the relatively primordial reality of Israel. They explain its acquisition of the land, archetypically, by revealing how it took place in the relative beginning, with the absolute beginning of the state. This archetype is not immutable. The events which it purports to explain are neither irreversible nor unique. The archetype undergoes modification because of its explanatory function. For the same reason the archetypical events are not irreversible, neither are they unique. The unique event is an unintelligible event. It becomes unintelligible by its relation to other events with common noumenal characteristics which render explanation possible.

That explanation is expressed in the archetype whose successive modifications subvert the apparent uniqueness of subsequent events of the configuration. By harmonizing them with the archetype, the changes in the archetype which are required by consistency, are effected. By these interactions and modifications, the configuration, including its archetype, represents an intelligible expression of reality at each succesive phase,[292] intelligible because consistent. Events may occur at different times, and in fact they do, but the determinants of the events which render them intelligible remain immutable and atemporal. Here again, the atemporality and absolute character of the entelechy from time to time require the modification of the archetype which expresses the ontology of which that objective entelechy is a part.[293] The phenomena occur in time, but the comprehension of the phenomena requires a noumenal interrelation of the phenomena deduced from an ontology which, by its nature, is atemporal and thus immutable. Because the sequence we have examined is an incipient and evolving sequence, the modifications effected to sustain the authority of the ontology expressed in the archetype are clearly visible. As new phenomena occur the archetype is modified accordingly, if the new phenomena

---

[292] D. N. Freedman, "The Biblical Idea of History," pp. 38-40.

[293] For relevant studies of time in the OT, see Marsch, *Fullness of Time*, pp. 158-159, 167, esp. Walther Eichrodt, "Heilserfahrung und Zeitverständnis im Alten Testament," *ThZ* 12 (1956), esp. p. 123; Thorlief Boman, *Das Hebräische Denken im Vergleich mit dem Griechischen* (4th ed.; Göttingen: Vandenhoek und Ruprecht, 1965), pp. 120, 123, 148-149, 180.

are incompatible with the archetype and its corresponding evolving configuration.[294]

Throughout the process, the retributive dimension of the ontology, which is also expressed in the archetype, undergoes those modifications which are required by the evolving course of relevant events, so that at each point in the evolution of that linear sequence the archetype appears to render an immutable paradigmatic explanation for the events of the evolving configuration. The objective entelechy of this process which successively reasserts increasingly comprehensive versions of the archetype is the proclivity of the ratiocinative faculty for a comprehensive and consistent explanation for reality, meaning, the visible phenomena of its immediate experience, together with the record of phenomena of the past, *i. e.,* for an ontology. Ontology implies necessity; either all the relevant phenomena occur because they are caused by the entelechy of the ontology in which case they occur by necessity and are thus intelligible; or, failing this, the phenomenal world is, as a whole, chaotic and hence unintelligible. Thus the otherwise chaotic world of phenomena is intelligible only in its causal relation to the noumenal entelechy of the linear process. Although its phenomena occur in a temporal linear phenomenal sequence, their intelligiblity requires their successive harmonization with the noumenal entelechy whose immutability is expressed in the archetype and its configuration. Without this reasserted consistency, reality remains inscrutable, and the intelligibility of the world, which implies necessity, is the logical prerequisite for any inquiry into the justice of the world, and the sphere of that inquiry is history.

---

[294] Problematic is the view of von Rad, modified somewhat in the course of his discussion, that in wisdom "Hebrew man examined his sphere of life closely for reliable orders and gathered together whatever could be expressed in the form of rules, but in history he came upon Yahweh's irreversible historical decrees, which certainly could not be expressed in the form of rules and which, at least at first sight, were actually unique in character. In the one case it was a question of stating what was eternally valid, of noting general human experiences, in the other, of occurrences which established unique political and cultic facts"; see his *Wisdom in Israel* (London: SMC, 1972), p. 289; and compare, R. Rendtdorff, "Geschichtliches und weisheitliches Denken im Alten Testament," in Donner, ed., *Beiträge zur Alttestamentlichen Theologie,* pp. 348-349, 351-352.

BIBLIOGRAPHY

Albrektson, D. *History and the Gods.* Lund: Gleerup, 1967.

Alt, Albrecht, "Die Deutung der Weltgeschichte im Alten Testament," in his *Grundzüge des Volkes Israel.* München: Beck, 1967.

Amsler, Samuel, "Les Deux Sources de la Théologie de l'Histoire dans l'Ancien Testament." *Revue de Théologie et de Philosophie* 19 (1969).

Andersen, Francis, & Freedman, David Noel. *Hosea: A New Translation with Introduction and Commentary. AB* 24. New York: Doubleday, 1980.

Anderson, G. W., ed. *Tradition and Interpretation.* Oxford: Clarendon Press, 1979.

Barth, K., "Zur Bedeutung der Wüstentradition." *VT Supp.* 15 (1966).

Beyerlin, Walter. *Origins and History of the Oldest Sinaitic Traditions,* trans. by S. Rudman. Oxford: Blackwell's, 1961.

Boling, Robert G. *Joshua: A New Translation with Notes and Commentary. AB* 6. New York: Doubleday, 1982.

——— . *Judges: Introduction, Translation, and Commentary. AB* 6a. New York: Doubleday, 1975.

Bowman, Thorlief. *Das Hebräische Denken im Vergleich mit dem Griechischen,* 4th ed. Göttingen: Vandenhoeck und Ruprecht, 1965.

Braulick, Georg. *Die Mittel Deuteronomischer Rhetorik: Erhoben aus Deuteronomium 4, 1-40. An Bib* 68. Rome: Biblical Institute Press, 1978.

Bright, John. *Covenant and Promise.* Philadelphia: Westminster, 1976.

Brueggemann, Walter, "The Kerygma of the Deuteronomistic Historian." *Interpretation* 22 (1968).

——— . *The Land: Place as Gift, Promise and Challenge in Biblical Faith.* Philadelphia: Fortress, 1977.

——— . *Tradition for Crisis: A Study in Hosea.* Richmond: John Knox, 1968.

Buis, Pierre, "Les Conflicts entre Moise et Israel dans Exode et Nombres." *VT* 28 (1978).

Burrows, Millar, "Ancient Israel," in Robert Dentan, ed., *The Idea of History in the Ancient Near East.* New Haven: Yale University Press, 1957.

Cancick, H. *Grundzüge der Hetheitischen und Alttestamentlichen Geschichtsschreibung und Historische Wahrheit.* *SBS* 48. Stuttgart: Katholisches Bibelwerk, 1970.

Childs, Brevard S. *The Book of Exodus: A Critical Theological Commentary.* *OTL.* Philadelphia: Westminster, 1974.

——— , "A Study of the Formula 'Until This Day.' " *JBL* 82 (1963).

Clapham, Lynn, "Mythopoetic Antecedents of the Biblical World-View and their Transformation in Early Israelite Thought," in Frank M. Cross, ed., *Magnalia Dei, The Mighty Acts of God: Essays on the Bible and Archeology in Memory of G. Ernest Wright.* New York: Doubleday, 1976.

Clements, R. E. *A Century of Old Testament Study.* London: Lutterworth, 1976.

——— . *Prophecy and Covenant.* *SBT* 43. Naperville: Allenson, 1965.

——— . *Prophecy and Tradition.* Atlanta: John Knox, 1975.

——— , "Review of R. Rendtorff, *Das Überlieferungsgeschichtliche Problem des Pentateuch.*" *Journal for the Study of the Old Testament* 3 (July, 1977).

Coats, George E. *Rebellion in the Wilderness: The Murmuring Motif in the Wilderness Tradition of the Old Testament.* Nashville: Abingdon, 1968.

——— , "The Wilderness Itinerary." *CBQ* 34 (1972).

——— , "The Yahwist as Theologian? A Critical Reflection." *Journal for the Study of the Old Testament* 3 (July, 1977).

Cross, Frank M. *Canaanite Myth and Hebrew Epic.* Cambridge: Harvard University Press, 1973.

Cullmann, O. *Salvation in History.* New York: Harper and Row, 1967.

Dahood, Mitchell. *The Psalms.* *AB* 16, 17, 18. New York: Doubleday, 1965.

Davies, G. H., "The Yahwistic Tradition in the Eighth Century Prophets," in H. R. Rowley, ed., *Studies in Old Testament Prophecy Presented to Professor Theodore H. Robinson.* Edinburgh: Clark, 1950.

de Vaux, Roland. *The Early History of Israel,* trans. by David Smith. Philadelphia: Westminster, 1978.

de Vries, S. J., "The Origin of the Murmuring Tradition." *JBL* 87 (1968).

de Vries, Simon. *Yesterday, Today and Tomorrow: Time and History in the Old Testament.* London: S.P.C.K., 1975.

Dietrich, W. *Prophetie und Geschichte: Eine Redaktionsgeschicht-liche Untersuchung zum Deuteronomistischen Geschichtswerk.* *FRLANT* 108; Göttingen: Vandenhoeck und Ruprecht, 1972.

Eichrodt, Walther, "Heilserfahrung und Zeitverständnis im Alten Testament." *ThZ* 12 (1956).

————. *The Theology of the Old Testament,* trans. by J. A. Baker. Philadelphia: Westminster, 1961.

Eissfeldt, Otto. *The Old Testament: An Introduction,* trans. Peter Ackroyd, ed. New York: Harper and Row, 1965.

Eliade, Mircea. *Myth and Reality,* trans. by Willard Trask. New York: Harper and Row, 1963

————. *The Myth of the Eternal Return,* trans. by Willard Trask. Princeton: Princeton University Press, 1954.

————. *Sacred and Profane,* trans. by Willard Trask. New York: Harper and Row, 1959.

Elliger, Karl, "Sinn und Ursprung der priesterlichen Geschichts-erzählung." *ZTK* 49 (1952).

Engnell, Ivan. *A Rigid Scrutiny: Critical Essays in the Old Testament.* Nashville: Abingdon, 1969.

Frankfurt, Henri. *The Intellectual Adventure of Ancient Man.* Chicago: University of Chicago Press, 1946.

Freedman, David Noel, "The Biblical Idea of History." *Interpretation* 21 (1967).

————, "The Deuteronomic History." *IDB Supp.* Nashville: Abingdon, 1976.

————, "Divine Names and Titles in Early Hebrew Poetry," in Frank M. Cross, ed., *Magnalia Dei, The Mighty Acts of God: Essays on the Bible and Archeology in Memory of G. Ernest Wright.* New York: Doubleday, 1976.

————, "Divine Commitment and Human Obligation: The Covenant Theme." *Interpretation* 18 (1964).

Fretheim, T. E., "Elohist," *IDB Supp.*

Fritz, Volkmar. *Israel in der Wüste: Traditionsgeschichtliche Untersuchungen der Wüstenüberlieferung des Jahwisten. MTS* 7. Marburg: Elwert, 1970.

————. *Tempel und Zelt: Studien zum Tempelbau in Israel und zu dem Zeitheiligtum der Priesterschrift. WMANT* 47. Neukirchen-Vlyun: Neukirchener Verlag, 1977.

Gese, Hartmut, "Bemerkungen zur Sinaitradition." *ZAW* 79 (1967).

————, "Erwägungen zur Einheit der biblischen Theologie." *ZTK* 67 (1970).

Gray, John. *I and II Kings: A Commentary. OTL.* Philadelphia: Westminster, 1974.

Habel, Norman. *Literary Criticism of the Old Testament.* Philadelphia: Fortress, 1971.

Henry, M. L. *Jahwist und Priesterschrift: Zwei Glaubenszeugnisse. Arbeiten zur Theologie,* Heft 3. Stuttgart: Calwer, 1960

Hölscher, G. *Geschichtsschreibung in Israel: Untersuchungen zum Jahwisten und Elohisten.* Lund: Gleerup, 1952.

Jenks, A. W. *The Elohist and North Israelite Traditions. JBL Mon Ser* 22. Missoula: Scholars Press, 1977.

Jepsen, A. *Die Quellen des Königsbuches.* Halle: Niemeyer, 1956.

Kaiser, Otto. *Introduction to the Old Testament,* trans. by John Sturdy. Minneapolis: Augsburg Publishing House, 1977.

Killian, R., "Die Priesterschrift—Hoffnung auf Heimkehr," in Josef Schreiner, ed., *Wort und Botschaft: Eine Theologische und Kritische Einführung in die Probleme des Alten Testaments.* Würzburg: Echter Verlag, 1967.

Knight, Douglas, ed. *Tradition and Theology in the Old Testament.* Philadelphia: Fortress, 1977.

Koch, Klaus. *The Growth of Biblical Tradition: The Form-Critical Method,* trans. by S. M. Cupitt. London: Black, 1969

Krause, H. K., "Gesetz und Geschichte," *Evangelische Theologie* 2 (1951-52).

Loersch, Sigrid. *Das Deuteronomium und seine Deutung. Stuttgarter Bibelstudien* 22. Stuttgart: Katholisches Bibelwerk, 1967.

Lohfink, Norbert, "Auslegung deuteronomischer Texte IV. Verkündigung des Hauptgebots in der jüngsten Schicht des Deuteronomiums (Dt 4, 1-40)." *Bibel und Leben* 5 (1964).

———, "Bilanz nach Katastrophe—Das Deuteronomistische Geschichtswerk," in Josef Schreiner, ed., *Wort und Botschaft.* Würzburg: Echter Verlag, 1967.

———, "Darstellungskunst und Theologie in Dtn 1, 6-31, 29." Biblica 51 (1969).

———. *Das Hauptgebot: Eine Untersuchung literarischer Einleitungsfragen zu Dtn. 5-11.* Rome: Instituto Biblico, 1963.

Malamat, A., "The Doctrine of Causality in Hittite and Biblical Historiography." *VT* 5 (1955).

Marsh, John. *The Fullness of Time.* New York: Harper and Row, 1952.

Mayes, A. D. H., "Deuteronomy 4 and the Literary Criticism of Deuteronomy." *JBL* 100 (1981).

Mays, James Luther. *Amos: A Commentary. OTL.* Philadelphia: Westminster, 1969.

⸻. *Hosea: A Commentary. OTL.* Philadelphia: Westminster, 1969.

McCarthy, D. J. *Old Testament Covenant: A Survey of Current Opinion.* Richmond: John Knox, 1972.

McEvenue, S. E. *The Narrative Style of the Priestly Writer. An Bib* 50. Rome: Biblical Institute Press, 1971.

⸻, "A Source-Critical Problem in Numbers 14:26-38." *Biblica* 43 (1962).

Mendenhall, George. *The Tenth Generation: The Origins of the Biblical Tradition.* Baltimore: Johns Hopkins University Press, 1973.

Mittmann, Siegfried. *Deuteronomium 1:1-6, 3; Literarkritisch und traditionsgeschichtlich untersucht. BZAW* 139. Berlin: de Gruyter, 1975.

Moran, W. L., "The End of the Unholy War and the Anti-Exodus," *Biblia* 44 (1963).

Mowinckel, Sigmund, "Israelite Historiography," in *Annual of the Swedish Theological Institute* (Stockholm: 1963).

Nicholson, E. W. *Exodus and Sinai in History and Tradition.* Richmond: John Knox, 1973.

⸻. *Deuteronomy and Tradition.* Philadelphia: Fortress, 1967.

North, Christopher. *The Old Testament Interpretation of History.* London: Epworth Press, 1946.

Noth, Martin. *Das Buch Joshua,* 2nd ed. *HAT* 7. Tübingen: Mohr, 1953.

⸻. *Exodus: A Commentary,* trans. by J. S. Bowden. *OTL.* Philadelphia: Westminster, 1962.

⸻, "Die Historisierung des Mythus im Alten Testament," in his *Gesammelte Studien.* München: Kaiser, 1957.

⸻. *A History of the Pentateuchal Traditions,* trans. by Bernard Anderson. Englewood-Cliffs: Prentice-Hall, 1972.

⸻. *The Laws in the Pentateuch and Other Essays,* trans. by D. R. AP-Thomas; Philadelphia: Fortress, 1966.

⸻. *Numbers: A Commentary,* trans. by J. S. Bowden. *OTL.* Philadelphia: Westminster, 1968.

⸻. *Überlieferungsgeschichtliche Studien,* 3rd ed. Tübingen: Niemeyer, 1967.

Osswald, Eva, "Alt-orientalische Parallelen zur Deuteronomistischen Geschichtsbetrachtung," *MIO* 15 (1969).

Pannenberg, Wolfart, "Redemptive Event and History," in Klaus Westermann, ed., *Essays in Old Testament Hermeneutics.* Richmond: John Knox, 1963.

Perlitt, Lothar. *Bundestheologie im Alten Testament.* WMANT 36. Neukirchen-Vlyun: Neukirchner Verlag, 1969.

Plöger, J. G. *Literarkritische, formgeschichtliche und stilkritische Untersuchungen Deuteronomium.* BBS 26. Bonn: Hanstein Verlag, 1967.

Radjawane, A. N., "Das Deuteronomistische Geschichtswerk: Ein Forschungsbericht." *Theologische Rundschau* 38 (1974).

Rendtorff, Rolf, "Geschichtliches und weisheitliches Denken im Alten Testament," in Herbert Donner, ed., *Beiträge zur Alttestamentlichen Theologie.* Göttingen: Vandenhoeck und Ruprecht, 1977.

————, "Pentateuchal Studies on the Move." *Journal for the Study of the Old Testament* 3 (July, 1977).

————. *Die Überlieferungsgeschichtlichen Probleme des Pentateuchs.* BZAW 147. Berlin: de Gruyter, 1977.

————, "The 'Yahwist' as Theologian? The Dilemma of Pentateuchal Criticism." *Journal for the Study of the Old Testament* 3 (July, 1977).

Ricoeur, Paul. *The Symbolism of Evil,* trans. by Emersen Buchanan. Boston: Beacon Press, 1967.

Roberts, J. J. M., "Myth Versus History." *CBQ* 38 (1976).

Robinson, H. Wheeler. *Corporate Personality in Ancient Israel,* rev. ed. Philadelphia: Fortress, 1980.

Ruppert, Lothar, "Der Jahwist—Künder der Heilgeschichte," in Josef Schreiner, ed., *Wort und Botschaft.* Würzburg: Echter Verlag, 1967.

Sackenfeld, A., "The Problem of Divine Forgiveness in Numbers 14." *CBQ* 37 (1975).

Schmid, Hans Heinrich, "In Search of New Approaches in Pentateuchal Research." *Journal for the Study of the Old Testament* 3 (July, 1977).

————. *Der Sogenannte Jahwist.* Zürich: Theologischer Verlag, 1976.

Schmidt, Werner, "Ein Theologe in Salomonischer Zeit? Plädoyer für den Jahwisten." *BZ* 25 (1981).

Schulte, Hanellis. *Die Entstehung der Geschichtsschreibung im Alten Israel.* BZAW 128. Berlin: De Gruyter, 1977.

Seeligmann, I. L., "Erkenntnis Gottes und Historisches Bewusstsein im Alten Israel," in Herbert Donner, ed., *Beiträge zur alttestamentlichen Theologie: Festschrift für Walther Zimmerli zum 70. Geburtstag.* Göttingen: Vandenhoeck und Ruprecht, 1977.

Seitz, G. *Redaktionsgeschichtliche Studien zum Deuteronomium.* *BWANT* 13. Stuttgart: Kohlhammer, 1971.

Shils, Edward. *Tradition.* Chicago: University of Chicago Press, 1981.

Smend, Rudolf. *Elemente alttestamentlichen Geschichtsdenkens.* *TS* 92. Zürich: EVZ, 1968.

————, "Das Gesetz und die Völker," in Hans Walter Wolff, ed., *Probleme Biblischer Theologie: Gerhard Rad zum 70. Geburtstag.* München: Kaiser, 1971.

Soggin, Alberto, "Deuteronomistische Geschichtsauslegung während des babylonischen Exils," in Felix Christ, ed., *Oikonomica: Heilsgeschichte als Thema der Theologie: Oscar Cullmann zum 65. Geburtstag gewidmet.* Hamburg-Bergstedt: Reich, 1967.

Soggin, J. A. *Joshua: A Commentary,* trans. by R. A. Wilson. *OTL.* Philadelphia: Westminster, 1962.

Speiser, E. A., "Ancient Mesopotamia," in R. Dentan, ed., *The Idea of History in the Ancient Near East.* New Haven: Yale University Press, 1955.

————, "The Biblical Idea of History in Its Common Near Eastern Setting." *Israel Exploration Journal* 7 (1957).

————. *Genesis: A Commentary. AB* 1. New York: Doubleday, 1964.

Stoebe, H. J., "Gut und Böse in der Jahwistischen Quelle des Pentateuchs." *ZAW* 65 (1954).

Thiel, W. *Die Deuteronomistische Redaktion von Jeremiah, 1-25.* *WMANT* 41. Neukirchen-Vluyn: Neukirchener Verlag, 1973.

Tunyogi, Andrew. *The Rebellions of Israel.* Richmond: John Knox, 1969.

van Seters, John, "The Yahwist as Theologian? A Response." *Journal for the Study of the Old Testament* 3 (July, 1977).

von Rad, Gerhard. *Deuteronomy: A Commentary,* trans. by Dorothea Barton. *OTL.* Philadelphia: Westminster, 1966.

————. *The Form Critical Problem of the Hextateuch and Other Essays,* trans. E. W. T. Dicken. New York: McGraw-Hill, 1966.

——— . *Old Testament Theology,* trans. by D. M. G. Stalker (2 vols.). New York: Harper and Row, 1962.

——— . *Wisdom in Israel,* trans. by James Q. Martin. London: SCM Press, 1972.

Vriezen, Th., "The Exegesis of Exodus XXIV, 9-11," in *The Witness of Tradition (Papers read at the Joint British-Dutch Old Testament Conference held at Woudschoten).* Leiden: Brill, 1972.

Wagner, Norman, "A Response to Professor Rolf Rendtorff." *Journal for the Study of the Old Testament* 3 (July, 1977).

Weimar, P. *Geschichten und Geschichte der Befreiung Israels.* Stuttgart: KBW, 1975.

Weinfeld, Moshe. *Deuteronomy and the Deuteronomic School.* New York: Oxford University Press, 1971.

——— , "The Period of the Conquest and the Judges as Seen by the Earlier and Later Sources." *VT* 17 (1967).

Weippert, Helga, "Die 'deuteronomistischen' Beurteilungen der Könige von Israel und Juda und das Problem der Redaktion der Königsbücher." *Biblica* 53 (1972).

Weippert, Manfred, "Fragen des israelitischen Geschichtsbewusstseins." *VT* 22 (1973).

Weiser, Arthur. *The Psalms: A Commentary,* trans. by Herbert Hartwell, *OTL.* Philadelphia: Westminster, 1961.

Weiser, Artur, "Glaube und Geschichte im Alten Testament," in his *Glauben und Geschichte im Alten Testament und andere ausgewählte Schriften.* Göttingen: Vandenhoek und Ruprecht, 1961.

——— . *The Old Testament: Its Formation and Development,* trans. by Dorothea Barton. New York: Association Press, 1961.

Wenham, G. J., "The Deuteronomic Theology of the Book of Joshua." *JBL* 90 (1971).

——— , "Review of H. H. Schmid, *Der Sogenannte Jahwist." Journal for the Study of the Old Testament* 3 (July, 1977).

Westermann, Claus, "Die Herrlichkeit Gottes in der Priester schrift." *Forschung im Alten Testament.* München: Kaiser, 1974.

——— . *The Promise to the Fathers,* trans. by David Green. Philadelphia: Fortress, 1980.

Whybray, R. N., "Response to Professor Rendtorff." *Journal for the Study of the Old Testament* 3 (July, 1977).

Wijngaards, J. N. M. "The Dramatization of Salvific History in the Deuteronomic Schools." *Oudtestamentische Studien* XVI. Leiden: Brill, 1969.

Wilcoxen, Jay, "Some Anthropocentric Aspects of Israel's Sacred History." *Journal of Religion* 48 (1968).

Wolff, Hans W. *Hosea: A Commentary,* trans. by Gary Stansell. Philadelphia: Fortress, 1974.

———, "Hosea's geistige Heimat," in his *Gesammelte Studien.* München: Kaiser, 1964.

———. *Joel and Amos,* trans. by W. Janzen. Philadelphia: Fortress, 1977.

———, "The Kerygma of the Yahwist," in Walter Brueggemann and Hans W. Wolff, eds., *The Vitality of Old Testament Traditions.* Atlanta: John Knox, 1975.

Zenger, E. *Die Sinaitheophanie: Untersuchungen zum jahwistischen und elohistischen Geschichtswerk. Forschung zur Bibel* 3. Würzburg: Echter, 1971.

Zimmerli, Walther. *The Law and the Prophets.* Oxford: Blackwell's, 1965.

———. *Ezekiel: A Commentary on Chapters 1-24,* trans. by R. E. Clements. Philadelphia: Fortress, 1979.

———. *Studien zur alttestamentlichen Theologie und Prophetie: Gesammelte Aufsätze II.* München: Kaiser, 1974.

Note on the Authors

David Noel Freedman is director of the Program on Studies in Religion in the University of Michigan, director of the W. F. Albright School of Archeological Research, Vice-President of the American Schools of Oriental Research, past-president of the Society for Biblical Literature, editor of the Anchor Bible series, editor of the *Bulletin of the American Schools of Oriental Research,* and author of numerous books and articles.

Richard Adamiak is a doctoral candidate in the University of Chicago. His articles have appeared in *The Journal of Politics, Journal of the History of Ideas,* and *Survey: A Journal of East and West Studies.*

DATE DUE

BRODART, INC.   Cat. No. 23-221